THE WILL OF GOD
IN AN UNWILLING WORLD

Other books by J. Ellsworth Kalas
from Westminster John Knox Press

Grace in a Tree Stump: Old Testament Stories of God's Love
Men Worth Knowing: Biblical Meditations for Daily Living
Preaching the Calendar: Celebrating Holidays and Holy Days

THE WILL OF GOD
IN AN UNWILLING WORLD

J. ELLSWORTH KALAS

WJK WESTMINSTER
JOHN KNOX PRESS
LOUISVILLE • KENTUCKY

First Edition
Published by Westminster John Knox Press
Louisville, Kentucky

11 12 13 14 15 16 17 18 19 20—10 9 8 7 6 5 4 3 2 1

Book design by Drew Stevens
Cover design by designpointinc.com
Cover art: © luismmolina/istockphoto.com

Library of Congress Cataloging-in-Publication Data

Kalas, J. Ellsworth
  The will of God in an unwilling world / J. Ellsworth Kalas. — 1st ed.
    p. cm.
  Includes bibliographical references and index.
  ISBN 978-0-664-23398-3 (alk. paper)
  1. God (Christianity)—Will. I. Title.
  BT135.K28 2011
  231.7—dc22

                                           2010037254

PRINTED IN THE UNITED STATES OF AMERICA

♾ The paper used in this publication meets the minimum requirements of the American National Standard for Information Sciences—Permanence of Paper for Printed Library Materials, ANSI Z39.48-1992

Westminster John Knox Press advocates the responsible use of our natural resources. The text paper of this book is made from 30% post-consumer waste.

To John Twist

In gratitude for the effort you have invested
in our friendship, and for the holy perception
with which you have prayed for me.

CONTENTS

PREFACE

When the writer of Ecclesiastes complained, "Of making many books there is no end," he may have been thinking especially of books that ask why things are as they are. Indeed, his own book is rather much on that theme, though he writes from the vantage point of disillusioned abundance, while most people voice their feelings on this subject from circumstances of loss: "Why does God allow (or cause) bad things to happen?"

So why am I attempting still another book on the subject?

Partly because several people whose judgment I otherwise trust have urged me to do so. And partly because in the nearly forty years that I was a pastor I faced the question so many times—sometimes philosophically from those who were simply angry with the way our world seems to operate, and more often from those who had encountered the questions at a personal, painful, sometimes tearful level.

In this book I have tried earnestly, as a fellow pilgrim, to look at several facets of the question. But I have concentrated especially on what our role may be in the issues of evil and the will of God. That is, I have worked less on the questions that sometimes lead nowhere and have concentrated instead on those elements in the discussion where we can make a difference, and where therefore we ought to try to do so.

I wish you Godspeed in the reading.

J. Ellsworth Kalas

Chapter 1
WHEN EVERYONE IS A THEOLOGIAN

Let me begin with a conclusion, or at least with something that affects my conclusions. I do this for reasons of full disclosure, so that you will know the prejudices with which I write. I believe that God's will for you and me is good. God's will for history is good. God's will for our planet is good. *Always.*

Of course we do not always see it that way, because, from where we sit, God's will is rarely simple. We should not expect it to be, since we play a strategic part in it, and you and I have a way of complicating life wherever we touch it. And of course God's will seems confusing because our experience with the will of God is always at some point where our time-bound wishes and perceptions intersect with God's eternal purposes. You and I are naturally inclined to be time bound in our attitudes and dreams, so we have a hard time being interested in God's eternal purposes, to say nothing of really grasping them.

And there is another problem. The times when we are most likely to be concerned about the will of God are those times when it is most difficult to be rational. Usually we become theologians in the midst of disaster—whether a flood, a hurricane, or a tsunami, on the one hand, or the death of a loved one, on the other. At such times few of us are equipped to reason out the purposes of God or even to determine if God has a purpose in what has happened. Of course, it is at just such times that we need most passionately to have answers, and it is at such times that we cobble together answers of our own, often with the well-intentioned help of someone given to superficial answers. Indeed, superficial answers have particular appeal when we are ready to settle for any philosophical port in the storm.

At times of personal or natural disaster the theologian that resides in every human rises up to ask, "Where was God in all of this?" or "Why does God allow things like this to happen?" And almost inevitably someone will be quick to answer, "It must have been the will of God, or else it wouldn't have happened."

Lynn Johnston's comic strip "For Better or Worse" put the matter in playful fashion. April, the daughter of the lead characters, had been bitterly opposed to her parents' buying a particular house, so opposed that she prayed that something would happen to prevent the purchase. When a storm felled a great tree on the house, April felt that she was guilty, since she had "put a curse" on the house. Her friend Eva reassured her that there is no such thing as curses. Eva then added brightly, "It was an act of God."[1] The cartoonist, Ms. Johnston, was handling the subject playfully, but she was also insightful: people who think themselves too intellectually sophisticated to believe in curses are quite comfortable making God the villain of all calamities. This attitude springs from our fatalistic feeling that whatever happens in our world—especially anything both disastrous and somewhat inexplicable—is ultimately planned by God, ordained by God, and thus, of course, God's will.

This kind of thinking is no respecter of wealth, position, education, or even of spirituality. It is as likely to be

heard in the vacation villa of the person who owns homes
in four or five locations as in the one-room ghetto shelter.
When tragedy comes, the people who ask, "Why?" say it
with surprisingly similar accents. Although education may
help a person couch the question in more sterile, detached
terms, such terms cannot completely eliminate a catch in
the throat.

At this point, as I have already said, everyone becomes
a practicing theologian. I think of a summer afternoon
many years ago when as a pastor I visited a husband and
wife who had no church affiliation but who had been convinced by one of my parishioners that perhaps I could help
them during what seemed a nearly hopeless time in their
lives. The middle-aged woman was dying slowly, steadily,
and painfully, and her husband—a rough-hewn man—had
all but quit his regular employment in order to take care of
her. Their apartment had touches that revealed the woman
had tried to make her house a home, but now the place was
marked by evidences that her inexpert husband had for
some time simply been seeking to hold things together.

I began our conversation cautiously and gently—
much as a good family doctor would begin a physical
examination—to examine their souls. I heard how long the
woman had been ill, her doctor's prognosis, and the report
that no alternatives remained. I learned too that the church
and references to God had not been part of their lives in their
adult years, and not much in any earlier period. But this did
not stop the husband from speaking as a theologian. After
his wife had summed up her story, her husband offered his
analysis. "As I said, I've never been much of a churchgoer,
but I can tell you this: If God won't do something for my
wife, then God can just go to hell." He was not trying to
shock me; he was only speaking as people will when they

are wounded to the depths of their souls. Nor was I upset by what he said or by the vehemence with which he said it. I told him that hundreds of years ago people had expressed essentially the same feelings and that you could find their words recorded in the Bible, particularly in some of the Psalms, at places in the book of Job, and in the writings of some of the Old Testament prophets.

At the time of the massive Indian Ocean tsunami, William Safire asked, "Where Was God?" in a column in the *New York Times*.[2] Safire, a thoughtful, incisive writer, quickly assumed the mantle of a theologian. In the third paragraph of his op-ed piece he wrote, "Turn to the Book of Job in the Hebrew Bible." You might have thought he was introducing the Scripture lesson for a service of worship rather than a reasoned investigation of headline news. His introduction was not misleading, because he then proceeded to give biblical insight into what had happened and how we might view God's part in the events. He argued, especially, that victims of any such catastrophe should not be seen as deserving their fate, that the Scriptures allow us to question God's part in our world, and that such questioning need not undermine faith. Significantly, Safire argued that humanity has an obligation to ameliorate injustice and that, in its response to the tsunami, humanity had done so with great generosity (a matter to which we shall return later).

I venture that the will of God is the most frequently discussed of all theological questions. Without doubt it excites and exercises more people than most of the questions that have shaped the great creedal statements—questions like the divine and human nature of Christ and the meaning of the Holy Trinity. In fact I suspect that the will of God is a more insistent and demanding question for the average person than even questions about the existence of

God—perhaps because, for a great many people, the existence of God becomes an issue only when a particular experience makes them wonder if there is a God and, if there is, what kind of character is at work in what is, at that moment, an irrational world. While a monstrous natural disaster or human-made annihilation generating headlines around the world may cause widespread theological reflection, those questions about headline events form only a tip of our theological iceberg. "Where was God?" is an everyday question, a question, in fact, for every hour and every minute of every day. When a person is killed by a drunken driver, when an errant baseball becomes as deadly as David's stone for Goliath, when a honeymoon or long-anticipated vacation is turned into a death trip: these events make us wonder if someone is throwing dice with our lives and our happiness.

The professional philosopher or theologian has a word for the kind of question to which I am referring: *theodicy*. This word means "a vindication of the divine attributes, particularly holiness and justice, in establishing or allowing the existence of physical and moral evil."[3] Theodicy asks, What do disasters large or small say about the character of God? How much is God involved in the evil that happens on our planet? Is God personally, directly involved—or is God simply indifferent? In either case, how can God be good when such un-good things are happening? Even though we have a philosophical word for this issue, and although that word may seem to elevate our discussion to a scholarly level, ultimately we *feel* the question more than we understand it, and no learned word changes that very human fact.

It is both very human and very natural to entertain such questions, and it is also very right to do so. Granted,

God is generally misrepresented in such discussions, not only by those who doubt God or see God as their enemy, but also—unfortunately—by some who seek to defend God. We would discuss God better at our times of extremity if we gave God more thought in ordinary times. I suspect, however, that only the most saintly of us use our best theological capacity at times other than tragedy. Perhaps this might be part of the definition of a saint: someone who thinks about God when not driven by circumstances to do so.

But surely, when life crashes in, there could be no bigger, more appropriate, or more insistent questions than these: Why do bad things happen? Why do they happen at given times or to certain people, while other times and other people seem to escape? Where does God fit into such a complex? If one argues that God is good and beautiful, as some of us devoutly believe, how does such beauty coexist with such manifest ugliness? Is the ugliness of our universe of such proportions as to overpower the good and beautiful?

At this point many persons come up with an answer that seems (for them) to put an end to debate or question. Whatever the tragedy, whether massive or private, they come eventually (and sometimes rather quickly) to an answer that is meant to put an end to further discussion: "It must have been the will of God." One finds this explanation in most of the world's religions in one form or another. One finds it too across the entire gamut of people who identify themselves as Christians, from the earnestly devout to the nominally religious, from those who see God in every part of life to those who usually are rather oblivious to God and religion. And the more inexplicable the situation or the more monstrous the happening, the more emphatically this explanation is likely to be expressed—almost as if the more difficult the question, the more certain the answer. A simple logic seems to be at work: if the question and the circumstances surrounding it are beyond comprehension, then we will find our explanation in that One who is beyond comprehension, namely, God. "It couldn't happen," someone says dismissively, "if it weren't God's will." For many, that settles the argument. What more can be said, once the name of God is invoked? What more needs to be said? At this point even the conventional doubter sees God as a kind of philosophical refuge, a kind of comfortable excuse for pursuing the issue no further.

For many, the statement "It was God's will" is a declaration of faith. Some of the most devout speak this position as the ultimate expression of their belief in God. It is their way of confessing that God is indeed omnipotent and therefore that whatever happens is within God's control. To question it in any way is to question God's wisdom and love and character; to probe any farther is to be irreverent and doubting.

I honor the earnestness of those who take this position because of their love of God. Indeed, some of the most admirable expressions of piety have come from people who work from such a theological base. In their devotion they find their way through any hardship, any physical affliction, any persecution or disappointment. They declare that whatever has happened is now their cross to bear, and they mean to bear it without complaint or question.

As much as I admire such expressions of faith and trust, I feel that these expressions may be a means of flight from reasoning, from wrestling with the problem. As I shall note later, I am thinking not simply of philosophical struggling, but more particularly of how we engage ourselves in the war between good and evil. I am troubled also that the answer which lays the whole burden on God forces us to another, even more troubling question: What kind of God would be party to such infinite pain? If this is, indeed, the nature of God, then ours is an irrational universe, and we should not be blamed for wanting to exit it as soon and as gracefully as possible.

Then comes still another issue: our human responsibility or, to put it more emphatically, our understanding of who and what we are as human creatures. The kind of thinking that concludes, "Whatever happens, it is God's will," allows us to abdicate any basic sense of moral requirement for life on this planet. After all, if God is the author of the disaster and pain, or if God has at the least acquiesced in it by not interfering, then how dare I complain? If I complain, I seem to be critiquing God or God's purposes. Worse still, if I involve myself too directly in finding a solution to the pain, it seems—logically speaking—that I am setting myself in opposition to God's will. This kind of reasoning makes God the only real actor in the drama of our universe; all the rest of us are pawns, waiting to be acted upon. Such reasoning insults God by making God seem capricious, as if God finds amusement in the struggles of creatures. Further, it insults what the Scriptures describe as God's highest creation, humanity, by making us ultimately helpless in the assignments God gave us when we were given dominion over this creation (Gen. 1:26–28).

Let me restate some of the bedrock conviction of this book. I do not believe that everything that happens on our planet or in our individual lives is the will of God. When I see evil in the world, whether or not I can locate its source, I feel like the landholder in Jesus' parable who found that tares were growing in his field of wheat: "An enemy has done this" (Matt. 13:28). If that is so, I am compelled by my love for God, for humanity, and for our planet to enter the conflict against this enemy. I will begin by searching my own conduct and my own soul to see if perhaps I am, wittingly or unwittingly, an accomplice of the enemy. One of the first acts in this self-search will be an examination of my own thinking: to what degree am I cooperating with evil by my attitude? By no means will I subscribe to the idea that everything that happens on our planet is God's will. I can hardly imagine a more profane, more obscene idea.

At the same time, I believe that God can bring the divine will to pass, regardless of the ugliness of any situation. I am confident that we humans can never make a mess so complicated, so contrary, or so obtuse that God cannot bring good out of it. I believe there is nothing in our universe so opposed to the will of God that God cannot reshape it into God's own ultimate purpose. This is the essence of the message in the book of Revelation, that in the consummation of all things God will bring about a new heaven and a new earth (Rev. 21:1) in which the eternal, sacred will is done.

While not everything that happens in our world is good, nevertheless, if you and I work with God, good will come from it. I am confident that no human wickedness or selfishness or stupidity or arrogance is so great that God cannot make it an instrument of goodness and redemption. I believe that God has chosen to work this consummate miracle with our help. Of all the creatures on this planet, only we human beings can get in the way of God's will, and only we can consciously participate in bringing God's will to pass.

I believe that you and I can—indeed, because we are human, that we *must*—enter the most barren and hopeless of humanity's struggles with the absolute certainty that

God, and all that is good, will eventually win. The final form of this victory, and of the conflict that leads to its consummation, is envisioned in the strangely triumphant language of the book of Revelation. This book was itself written in the midst of hellish times. This fact makes its message all the more authentic. I suspect that if we read Revelation in the light of those questions that seem to us to be most morally wrenching, we may find it easier to understand (at least emotionally) those chapters that are so graphic in their description of the destruction wrought both by evil itself and by God's judgment upon evil. The writer of Revelation hopes that we will grasp the degree to which our world is out of joint. This out-of-jointness is so monstrous that when God brings it to order and ultimate rightness, the process is itself terrifying to behold.

I have still another faith. I believe not only that God and goodness will eventually win, both on this planet and in eternity, and not only that you and I are factors in this battle for the will of God, but something still more astonishing: that we—you and I!—are the key players in bringing to pass God's perfect will in our obviously imperfect, demonstrably unwilling world. To be part of such an eternal plot is to understand with new passion what the Scriptures mean when they say that we are "fearfully and wonderfully made" (Ps. 139:14). What is more fearful than that we should have a role in life's most demanding question, more wonderful than that we ultimately can help tilt the scales?

Before we get into such matters of holy challenge, let us ask ourselves how our world became the seeming enigma that we know it to be.

Chapter 2

A WORLD OUT OF JOINT

Both critics and general readers would agree that Joseph Heller's most significant novel was *Catch 22*; it has even given a defining phrase to our common speech, an achievement rare for any piece of literature. My personal philosophical kinship with Heller, however, comes with a less well-known novel, one that takes its title from the opening sentence of the second paragraph of the book: "Something must have happened to me sometime."[1]

I am altogether sure that "something must have happened"—not only to the lead character in Heller's novel or to me as an individual or to any number of individuals like me, but to our whole human race. Yes, and even to our planet. Clearly, something in our world is out of joint. In most respects, almost all of the time, ours is a clockwork universe, astonishing in its precision. Then the irrational bursts in like darkness at midday, and we are pained again to see that we live in a world that is out of joint.

When I speak of the precision and predictability of our universe, I am including—believe it or not—the actions and conduct of us human creatures. We are the most unpredictable element in this universe, the element that makes gamblers want to set odds, because we are the choice makers; we don't operate as if we were programmed—because, in fact, we are not. Nevertheless, one can set quite sure odds on our human conduct, and most of the time the odds are on the side of what is good. The news media reason that only bad news is real news, because what is bad is out of the ordinary, while what is good is predictable and likely. The late-night news spends a good deal of time on house fires because only a miniscule percentage of houses burn in any given day or even in any year. The media report crimes and accidents because they are not the norm. When you observe life objectively, you realize that the norm is *good* and that the bad is relatively rare.

Some individuals will argue from their own experience or from the experience of someone close to them that this is not true. From my own observation of certain especially unfortunate persons, I acknowledge the point these persons want to make. All of us know someone whose life seems to have suffered more ill than good, and for such persons I have nothing but compassion and prayer, and also a feeling it is not right that their path should be so much more anguished than mine. But it is the scarcity of such cases that brings them so forcibly to mind. I will agree too that there have been periods in history when tragedy seemed to dominate, and there are nations or regions where evil seems more largely in control, whether by natural disasters or by malevolent governments. But here too these times and places assert themselves in our minds, not because they are so prevalent, but because they are comparatively rare.

But we are brought back to the insistent question: Why is there evil, why are there disasters? Why should there be *any* evil, *any* irrational pain, or *any* destructive conduct? The pain that invades our world is so disruptive that it succeeds at times in clouding out the sunlight. How can this be? Was our world meant to be out of joint? Or has "something happened"?

I submit that our world was meant to operate flaw-lessly. I confess again, for purposes of full disclosure, that I start with a prejudice. My prejudice is laid out in classical form in the stories of creation in chapters 1–3 of the book of Genesis. Let me quickly note that the Genesis creation sto-ries are not as concerned with matters of science as with an understanding of the wonders of life, particularly the won-ders of life as lived with God. The Genesis 1 description of a process of creation is almost incidental to its declara-tion of the heart behind the process. Thus, at regular and repeated intervals in the story, the writer tells us that the Creator was pleased with what was unfolding; the Creator saw that it was *good*, and near the end of the creation event, it was in fact *very good*. This goodness pleased the Creator. The project was just what it ought to be, and it was time for the Sabbath, the unique rest for work well done.

Then, something happened. Genesis 3 tells us it hap-pened, of all things, at the very center of unequalled beauty, in a garden called Eden, the place of perfection—the crown jewel in a setting of the utterly exquisite. This suggests that there is no setting so beautiful as to be immune to ugliness, no garden so perfect that evil cannot intrude. And the entry point of evil is found in the most responsible personality in all of the creation, the human being. To add an exclama-tion mark to the point, the locus of the human failure is in the quality of personality that is most dramatically human, the power of *choice*. From all we can observe (and surely research never ceases to seek both similarities and differ-ences between us and the rest of creation), no other crea-ture makes moral choices in the same way humans do.

Further, as the Genesis narrator makes clear, the choice is made via the wonderful human gift of reason. The people in the garden do not act out of instinct or intuition, but out of reason: when the prospect of the forbidden fruit was presented to her, "the woman saw that the tree was good for food, and that it was a delight to the eyes, and that the tree was to be desired to make one wise" (Gen. 3:6). The human creature is strategically equipped to make decisions, for the physical necessities of life ("good for food") and for the aesthetic qualities that give us sophistication ("a delight to the eyes"), and is empowered with the intelligence—depending on how we use it!—to enrich or impoverish our planet.

They chose, this remarkable couple; and all of us ever since, whether remarkable or ordinary, have continued to choose. By their choice, as Genesis reports it, we have been left with a planet where "something must have happened"—and worse, where it happens still.

But how exactly did it happen? Genesis tells us that the man and the woman had been warned that their paradise had one—just one—absolutely crucial issue. They were forbidden to eat the fruit of one particular tree. If the managers of the garden took from that tree, they would die. If we follow the story to some logical premise, we figure that "to die" was not conceivable to this man and woman, so they were not frightened by the threatened consequences. This should not surprise us, because after untold generations of the human story, consequences still do not sufficiently impress us so that we decide to change our conduct. This is true whether the issue is as personal as the perils of an unhealthy lifestyle or as planet shaping as global warming or atomic destruction. We seem always to be quite sure that the consequences won't apply to us—or in matters of mass peril, to our generation or that of our children.

Genesis 3 tells the story in a kind of fable fashion. A serpent—"more crafty than any other wild animal that the

Lord God had made"—came to the couple with a question (a quite philosophical one: is God good?) and involved them in a conversation. It was an intriguing subject, and before they knew it, the couple had broken the only commandment they had received; they had eaten of the forbidden fruit (Gen. 3:1–6).

The Bible doesn't answer several questions that really trouble us. It doesn't say who this serpent was, or how he happened to be in the garden of perfection when he was the kind of creature that would raise questions about the character of God. Nor does it tell us how he got to be that way. Worse yet, Genesis doesn't tell us why God didn't obliterate the instigator of this tragic conversation. True, the serpent hears that he is now "cursed . . . among all wild creatures; upon your belly you shall go, and dust you shall eat all the days of your life" (Gen. 3:14). Nevertheless, he is not annihilated for what he has done.

Dietrich Bonhoeffer was a person who knew something about evil. Because his father was a psychiatrist and Dietrich a careful listener to dinner table conversation, I suspect that he began early to observe human behavior with a sophisticated eye. As a theologian, he looked at life and people through the perceptive lens of Scripture. By growing up in Germany in the tumultuous 1920s and 1930s, he was exposed to a culture in which conventionally religious voices seemed tentative and ineffective, while political voices became ever more insistent. Then evil found a startling, dramatic voice in the Nazi movement and Adolf Hitler. Dietrich Bonhoeffer became a perceptive observer of that evil, one of its most courageous opponents, and eventually, in his martyrdom, its victim.

When Bonhoeffer tried to explain the nature of evil, he wrote, "The Bible does not claim to provide information regarding the origin of evil but to bear witness to its character as guilt and as unending human burden."[2] He emphasized that we humans—"the creature of God"— have done the evil. Working from a biblical point of view, Bonhoeffer did not blame evil on particular movements or particular people, though certainly he had convincing examples in Hitler, the Nazi movement, the people who supported the Nazis, and the shortcomings of the German state church. Instead, he concentrated on the fact that all we humans, we creatures of God, have done the evil. More than that, with an extraordinary sense of his role as a human being, Bonhoeffer insisted on taking the responsibility personally: "I have done evil—something entirely against God."[3]

In this response, Bonhoeffer improved significantly on Adam and Eve. When God confronted them after their sin, the errant couple promptly began to make excuses and to look for someone to blame. Adam blamed Eve (and also God, describing Eve as "the woman you gave to be with me," as if he would never have been in this trouble if it weren't for God's giving him "the woman"), and Eve in turn blamed the serpent (Gen. 3:12–13). That the serpent made no such defense may well distinguish him from us humans, because we have a remarkable penchant for deflecting our failures onto someone else and thereby excusing ourselves from dealing with them.

Like every other human, I wish there were more answers to some of life's perplexing questions, but I think two questions are prior to the "Why?" question. First, following Bonhoeffer, in what ways am I, perhaps, responsible for the troubles that exist? Second, regardless of who or what is responsible, what can I do to alleviate the problem and to find some answers?

I believe that our universe is out of joint morally, because its principal actors—and the only ones, it seems, who have a controlling part—have broken, and continue to break, the moral code. I believe that this broken morality has affected all the structures and relationships of our planet. I say this out of the conviction that our planet operates according to moral rules, because it is the handiwork of a moral God. When we humans violate these rules, we cause a dissonance throughout the system.

The Hebrew prophets envisioned a perfect day yet to come; they saw a complete revolution in all our planet's parts. At the level of human security, the prophet Zechariah envisioned: "Old men and old women shall again sit in the streets of Jerusalem, each with staff in hand because of their great age. And the streets of the city shall be full of boys and girls playing in its streets" (Zech. 8:4–5). The prophet is describing a way of life so moral that two of its most helpless groups, the very young and the very old, inhabit its streets without fear—indeed, with pleasure and security.

The prophets saw more than civic and political renewal. They envisioned renewal at the very heart of creation. Thus Isaiah said,

> The wolf shall live with the lamb,
>   the leopard shall lie down with the kid,
> the calf and the lion and the fatling together,
>   and a little child shall lead them.
> The cow and the bear shall graze,
>   their young shall lie down together;
>   and the lion shall eat straw like the ox.
> The nursing child shall play over the hole of the asp,
>   and the weaned child shall put its hand on the
>   adder's den.

They will not hurt or destroy
  on all my holy mountain;
for the earth will be full of the knowledge of the
  LORD
  as the waters cover the sea."

Isa. 11:6–9

The prophet Hosea offered the same vision of a redeemed creation. "I will make for you a covenant on that day with the wild animals, the birds of the air, and the creeping things of the ground; and I will abolish the bow, the sword, and war from the land; and I will make you lie down in safety" (Hos. 2:18). Clearly these great inspired souls saw a connection between the conduct of us human beings and the state of the wider world of nature.

We can dismiss this thinking, at the worst, as the uninformed enthusiasm of the prescientific mind or, at best, as the poetic insights of a devout soul. But perhaps there is more to it. Now that we are recognizing how the style and extent of our uses of this planet's resources are affecting the balances of nature in ways that will in time change and imperil life as we know it, we should be better prepared to see how our human conduct affects not only our human relationships but the world of nature. At the least we should have our minds open to the possibility that there is something so profoundly spiritual about our world that our spiritual conduct—that is, our relationship with right and wrong, with justice and injustice, with love and hate—impacts nature itself. If we believe that God is indeed just and loving, and that our God-ordained universe should reflect this, then we have reason to ponder the relationship of our conduct and our thinking to the planet on which we live. We should ask ourselves how much of the suffering that exists in our world may have been caused or continues to be caused by our human conduct. But before getting too involved in such philosophical questioning, we need to ask ourselves how much of this suffering we can relieve or even eliminate by our positive involvement in the planet's enterprise.

It is very clear that "something has happened" on our planet. In our human relationships, the Adam who once saw his Eve as "bone of my bones and flesh of my flesh" (Gen. 2:23) now sees her as "the woman whom you gave to be with me" (Gen. 3:12). The ground that was a garden of paradise is now a place where there will be "thorns and thistles," and the human creature is told, "By the sweat of your face you shall eat bread" (Gen. 3:18–19).

Jesus told a story about the kingdom of heaven— which is to say, a story about the world as God wants it to be. In the story a landowner "sowed good seed in his field" (Matt. 13:24). (Let me interrupt the story to note that this portrayal of God—the landowner—is consistent with my conviction in this book: God is good, and God's intentions for our planet and for our individual lives are good. God sows *good* seed, with the intention of good results.) But "while everybody was asleep, an enemy came and sowed weeds among the wheat, and then went away" (Matt. 13:25). Predictably, as the seeds matured, the workers found a mixture of wheat and weeds. The workers were troubled; they explained to their employer that they sowed good seed and asked, "Where, then, did these weeds come from?" (Matt. 13:27).

The owner's answer was matter of fact and to the point: "An enemy has done this" (Matt. 13:28). The owner—apparently to the workers' surprise and sometimes, I think, to ours—was unhurried about remedying the matter. He explained the hazard of rooting out the weeds at this point, lest wheat be destroyed along with them. I don't want to press the details of a parable too far, but I think I'm justified at this point in reminding us that sometimes when we are impatient with what happens in our world and we then question God's interest or involvement, we might consider that perhaps the Landowner knows some things we do not.

Jesus' disciples were fascinated with this story and asked him later, privately, for an explanation. "The one who sows the good seed," Jesus explained, "is the Son of Man; the field is the world, and the good seed are the children of the kingdom; the weeds are the children of the evil one, and the enemy who sowed them is the devil" (Matt. 13:37–39).

Jesus did not bother to answer several questions that may trouble us. He did not tell us why there is evil. Evil exists and Jesus takes its reality as a given. Neither did Jesus explain who or what the "devil" is. The reality of evil remains the same, whatever name is employed. Jesus did assure us, however, that someday everything will be set right.

But for now it is clear that something must have happened. Things are not as they ought to be. Jesus says that the Landowner urges patience from his workers, but he does not suggest that the conditions in the field—all the weeds of life!—are God's will or that God likes it that way. Not so! "An enemy has done this." If this is the case, we would do well to learn more about the enemy, so that, at the very least, we do not find ourselves among his accomplices.

Chapter 3
OUR UNWILLING WORLD

Whether we are shoppers in the mall or scholars in the library stacks, we humans will probably discuss forever where evil came from and why it is allowed to exist. Few will argue about its reality. We may not be able to define evil satisfactorily, but we know it as a fact. We encounter it daily—in personal struggles, in community life, in world affairs. We know about it because it clamors for our attention, whether on the television screen, in the learned journal, in an idle conversation. If God, indeed, has a will for our world, there is certainly a force in our world that is unwilling.

Eugene Peterson, Bible translator and practicing theologian, puts the issue sharply:

> There is a spiritual war in progress, an all-out moral battle. There is evil and cruelty, unhappiness and illness. There is superstition and ignorance, brutality and pain. God is in continuous and energetic battle against all of it.
>
> God is for life and against death. God is for love and against hate. God is for hope and against despair. God is for heaven and against hell. There is no neutral ground in the universe. Every square foot of space is contested.[1]

Which is to say, we have an enemy. As surely as there is goodness in our world, there is something that opposes goodness. When we are sensitive to the issue of good and evil, we will agree with Peterson that "every square foot of space is contested." We are, indeed, in some kind of warfare, an unceasing struggle between good and evil.

Most of us have, at one time or another, confronted evil at a level where it is almost physical. We feel it. We think that in some measure we understand what Jesus experienced when in Gethsemane, according to Lukan tradition, his wrestling with evil was so real that his sweat was drops of blood (Luke 22:44). Our novelists, playwrights, and movie makers sometimes penetrate the heart of evil with more imagination and intensity than the preacher and the theologian. Perhaps this is because the preacher finds it too easy to quote familiar biblical and theological phrases without plumbing their meaning, while the novelist or playwright plunges into the subject without prior boundaries and without established vocabulary. Established vocabulary is convenient for discussion, but it also can hamper thinking.

We know that evil is there. If we forget the monstrous quality of evil, tonight's newscast will likely report some action, even within our own city or county, that lets us know how completely we humans can sell out to utter darkness. Of course, at times, history puts the data into a permanent record. Adolf Eichmann, while awaiting trial for his key part in some of the most horrendous acts of the Holocaust, said, "To sum it all up, I must say I regret nothing."[2] We think it impossible that someone could participate in evil as fully as Eichmann did and emerge with no sense of regret. But as we ponder Eichmann's public screen, we realize that he is only our own soul, writ large and ugly. Most of us can

recall times when, on a much smaller scale, we have acted
unkindly and destructively; not only do we not regret it, we
acknowledge that we would follow the same course again.
Often, in fact, we delight in telling our friends the exact
words we used to hurt the other person, as if our rejoinder
was a piece of literature.

So we need no proof that evil exists. Nothing could
be less necessary of proof. But what *is* evil? Is it a quality
that has somehow been let loose in our world that now func-
tions like a self-perpetuating board of directors that elects
for each generation a body to succeed itself? When so many
of us despise evil and the rest of us simply fear it, how does
it manage to continue to exist—and even to prosper?

Of course most of us are not involved in the scale of
evil that Eichmann represents. We are simpler folks, with no
intention of becoming part of some national or international
political or social movement dedicated to the destruction
of a particular people. Most of us exercise evil on a small
stage. But if we could put our little exercises of evil under
some kind of spiritual magnifying glass, we might discover
that it is like the infinitesimal insect living on an eyelash; our
evil is as monstrous if we could imagine it full size.

Occasionally a playwright or a novelist (for example,
Flannery O'Connor) portrays an individual who, within
his or her own family or community, is as malevolent as a
national dictator. Often enough, those living with such a
person will defend him or her with an argument like the
defenses made for Hitler and Mussolini, when people
pointed out they could not have been all bad, because they
created a punctual railway or effective highway system. The
only difference in the evil perpetrated by Hitler or Mussolini is the dimensions of its power and thus the scope of the
harm it caused. In principle, the evil is the same.

Of course most of us encounter evil in our personal experience at a less frightening level. Ironically, the less overt evil seems, the more its power is enhanced in our own lives. C. S. Lewis portrayed the issue in an almost playful way in *The Screwtape Letters*, in which a fictional devil's apprentice subtly leads his human victim astray with seemingly harmless suggestions. Those who read *Screwtape* thoughtfully become more sensitive to the functioning of evil in their everyday lives. Evil would not have a chance if its arguments did not edge so close to truth, and if they weren't so appealing to our minds and our emotions.

We will never know how to deal with evil in our world or in our own lives until we see how erratically the thread of evil picks its way through our good intentions. Blaise Pascal, a man of scientific genius, was also a person of profound Christian faith. He observed, "Men never do evil so completely and cheerfully as when they do it from religious conviction."[3] I know this is true, and I find it frightening. But I also find it altogether logical. In a distressing way, it demonstrates the good that is in us. Most humans wouldn't think of doing ill if they couldn't find a good (and by this I do, indeed, mean *good*, rather than logical) reason for doing it.

This is true at every level of life. I traveled through several countries of Africa in September 1961. Those countries were full of hope at the time. It was heartwarming to talk with young Africans where they expected soon to be free of colonial control, to be self-governing nations. They enjoyed talking with Americans, so they could lay their dreams alongside what they perceived to be dreams fulfilled in the American story. Now, half a century later, one sees two generations of shattered dreams in Africa. I think of Josiah Kariuki. As we talked on a flight from Ethiopia to Kenya, his passion and idealism made me wish I could come to Kenya to work with him for the future of his country. Just a few years later, he was assassinated by political opponents. I don't know who those assassins were, but I am quite sure they too were idealistic in their own way.

When I see the annual lists of the world's worst dictators, several are always from Africa. And because I remember the Africa of 1961, I know that these dictators had wonderfully idealistic soil in which to develop their power—but I'm almost equally sure that the dictators themselves have operated with their own sense of idealism. Of course the idealism of the dictator is mixed with arrogance and selfish ambition, but few if any dictators—and few if any perpetrators of evil at any level—will confess to pure cynicism as their motivation or their governing mood. We humans like to think that we do what we do because we want to do good. This fact is a testimony to the power of good and to evil's acknowledgment of that power; evil knows that it must rely on good for its excuse for existence.

We humans are capable not only of resisting God's goodness; far worse, we are capable of persuading ourselves that God is with us in our resistance. C. S. Lewis wrote a letter to Arthur Greeves, dated November 5, 1933, in which he said Adolf Hitler had claimed that the Jews have made no contribution to human culture and that, in crushing them, he was doing the will of the Lord.[4] These words sound like blasphemy to our ears, but I suspect that equally outrageous things—though not from such a well-known source—have been said tens of thousands of times. It is rare for anyone in public or private life to be as perceptive of his or her own frailty in matters relating to the will of God as Abraham Lincoln demonstrated in his second inaugural address. At that crucial point of history—crucial not

only to American political history but to moral history—
Mr. Lincoln said of the two sides in the Civil War that both
sides read the same Bible and pray to the same God, and
each invokes God's aid against the other.[5]

When we come to feel strongly about some moral,
civic, or political issue, we quickly anoint that issue with
divine favor.

Up to this point I have not tried to go further in
defining evil in either its source or its continuing center of
power. Personally, I am satisfied with the insights I find in
the Scriptures of the Old and New Testament. I sometimes
wish they were less enigmatic in their details, but since they
are what they are, I am dedicating myself in this book to
our human side of the story, that is, the part we play in evil
and the part we can play in countering it. Our natural—and
rather admirable—curiosity about evil's origin and locus
has tended to divert too many of us from enlisting more
vigorously in the struggle against evil at the levels where
we encounter it and where we can do so much to defeat
it. One does not have to understand the operations of the
enemy's military geniuses in order to protect one's own village. For now, I mean to deal with what I do understand,
and to do what I can about the area of my understanding.
What I understand is that I am capable both of being part of
the problem and of being part of the solution. Even when I
work hard to be part of the solution, I am always in danger
of slipping unconsciously into the camp of the problem—
even if only temporarily.

Sometimes when I hear people speak sadly of how
the devil is at work in our world, I think that we hardly need
a devil; we humans cause enough trouble unaided. We find
so many ways to make trouble. We do it through the body
politic, sometimes by neglecting the gift of democracy and

sometimes by misusing that gift. We do it through our corporate ventures, from our neighborhood associations, where we organize for good but then use the same devices to hurt, to our financial power, where we use corporations to do what many of us would not think of doing on a first-hand, one-on-one basis. We do it with human selfishness and with human profligacy.

Perhaps it is in self-defense that we so often ask the wrong question. At the time of the 2006 Sago Mine disaster, some reporters were asking theologians how God allows such tragedies to happen. Cathleen Falsani, religion writer with the *Chicago Sun-Times,* talked rather with Studs Terkel, who by then was in his nineties and had watched a lot of life go by. He told Ms. Falsani that God had not let the miners down, but that their employer had: "It's not an act of God, it's an act of guys—guys exploiting other guys!"[6] The Sago Mine had been cited repeatedly for safety violations more than 200 times in the year before the disaster.[7]

The circle widens. Has a government agency failed, in not following through on such warnings to see if changes are being made? Has Congress failed, in not providing enough financing to make such follow-through possible? In many corporate ventures, have stockholders failed, in not insisting that their companies be run honorably? Do stockholders sometimes care only about dividends, without asking how the money for those dividends is earned? Who needs a devil, when we humans so carelessly go on our way, making disaster possible, sometimes by our support of irresponsible conduct and sometimes by our silence and our indifference.

Arthur Miller made the point poignantly just after World War II in his play *All My Sons.*[8] It is the story of a manufacturer of substandard, defective war materials that cause the deaths of fliers during the war—including the manufacturer's own son. Of course (as the manufacturer eventually realizes over the course of the play), if we have regard for the human race, they are *all* our children. We hardly dare ask why *God* allows a specific plane to be shot down or to fail. We should ask, rather, what part we humans play in the tragedies that baffle us, tragedies that ought to stir us to action.

J. B. Phillips, the Anglican priest and scholar who blessed millions in the mid-twentieth century with his modern-language translation of the New Testament, threw out a kind of challenge to those who put the burden of the world's misery on God: "If we knew all the facts, and the effects, both short-term and long-term of human selfishness and evil, a very large proportion of mankind's miseries could be explained."[9] Let us begin with the assumption, one supported by the Scriptures and by common sense, that every human being should have as good a life as possible. That means that every person's right to such a life is as worthy as yours or mine.

It soon becomes clear that not everyone believes that; or if they do, some people do not follow through and apply this belief in their business or professional lives. A great many of us want money enough and power enough to have the advantage over other people and thus to control their lives in some measure. Indeed, by the distribution of talents—and especially by the way those talents are rewarded in the marketplace—some persons are placed in positions of superior power or influence. I am not so idealistic or so naive as to argue with this fact.

Unfortunately, this issue of power and control gets out of control very quickly. The person with power realizes that if those working for him or her are paid less, the profits are greater. It is easy to rationalize that he or she deserves this advantage. For most of human history, there are have been some people who have carried this idea still farther and have made other human beings their slaves, having concluded that those who are slaves are not fully human.

Of course we do not have to go to the marketplace to see how easy it is to for humans to make life less enjoyable for other humans. There seems to be something in all humans that makes us want to feel superior to someone else. Some exercise this desire in their home, among siblings or other family members; in some homes this is a continual conflict, a little war with its shrapnel and sniper attacks. Others find their opportunity at the checkout counter or with the server in the restaurant. It is easy for a teacher or a preacher to use the power of the podium to assert superiority, or for the doctor or lawyer to do so from their positions of professional authority. All of us have our opportunities to make life unpleasant, even miserable, for others or to diminish their sense of worth and importance.

If you believe, as I do, that God's purpose is to bless this planet and humanity—and indeed, all the rest of the creation—then it is incumbent upon us to cooperate with that idea and to seek in every way possible to fulfill the planet's potential for goodness, beauty, and grandeur of life for everyone.

Some of the pain in our world is altogether beyond my control, at least as far as I know. I can't prevent a tsunami or a hurricane or a flood. However, I can participate in endeavors that make people less susceptible to such tragedies. In truth, most of the pain in our world is not caused by acts of nature; most of it is caused by human beings, large and small, powerful and relatively insignificant, who bring hurt to other human beings.

So if God's will for our world is good—as I believe that it is and as I'm confident you also believe, except in times of life's distortions—then the question is this: How do I participate in the struggle between good and evil? Am I on God's side in this conflict? We are compelled to take sides. I cannot be an innocent bystander in this battle. Martin Luther King was right: "He who passively accepts evil is as much involved in it as he who helps to perpetuate it."[10]

Ultimately, the battlefield on which the issue of the will of God is being decided is the individual human soul. We see the conflict in its most dramatic forms in international warfare and in the halls of power, whether in the financial capitals of the world or in the political arenas. But all of these battlefields are secondary. Ultimately, we human beings vote for or against the will of God. We do so not only for the will of God in our own lives, but also for the lives of great numbers of persons who in one fashion or another come into our realm of influence.

If the perfect will of God is to be done in our imperfect world, you and I will play our own strategic role. We cannot escape it.

Chapter 4

WHEN GOOD COMES OUT
OF EVIL

If there is something in our world that opposes the will of God, there is surely goodness in our world that supports the will of God and asserts itself unceasingly. No matter how great the evil, no matter how deeply it seems to be entrenched, no matter how arrogantly evil asserts itself, the will of God is the ultimate phoenix, rising always out of the ashes of burnt-out evil.

Julian of Norwich lived in a time when evil declared itself in one of its most monstrous forms, the Black Death, in the fourteenth century. The plague killed between one-third and two-thirds of the population of Europe.[1] Those who lived at such a time must surely have thought that the world was coming to an end. In our contemporary world, when epidemics or pandemics strike, modern science quickly seeks its source and then begins working toward the plague's control and the cure of its victims. There was no such prospect of deliverance in Lady Julian's time. Nor could any assurance be given when she herself went through a period of severe illness. Yet she was confident that "all shall be well and all shall be well and all manner of thing shall be well."[2] As Darryl Tippens puts it, Lady Julian "came to an absolute conviction that every evil would be turned to good through God's miraculous work."[3]

This is the overwhelming mood of Scripture. When tragedy and shame strike the first family in Cain's murder of his brother, it seems that the purposes of God have been thwarted, because the victim, Abel, was the one whose offering God regarded, while God disregarded Cain's (Gen. 4:4–5). God answers the loss of Abel by giving Adam and Eve another son, Seth, who would become the ancestor of Noah, a man of righteousness through whom God brought redemption to the world.

When the wickedness of humankind was so great that "every inclination of the thoughts of their hearts was only evil continually," God found a man, Noah, who was "a righteous man, blameless in his generation" (Gen. 6:5, 9b). When the plot line seemed lost between confusion and deadly routine, God laid a hand upon Abram, a man who would punctuate his life's journey by building altars of gratitude and of new commitment (Gen. 12:1–8).

The principle is enunciated most succinctly, however, in the story of Joseph and his brothers (Gen. 37–50). The resentment the older brothers felt toward Joseph became so intense that they wanted nothing so much as to be rid of him; so when the opportunity came, they sold him into slavery (Gen. 37:17b–28). Roughly two decades later, they not only reconnected, but Joseph was now in a position of absolute power from which he could get full revenge for the harm his brothers had inflicted on him so many years before. When the brothers pleaded for mercy, Joseph explained how he understood what had happened: "Even though you intended to do harm to me, God intended it for good, in order to preserve a numerous people, as he is doing today" (Gen. 50:20).

I would like to write Joseph's statement across all the pages of human history. There are always those who use whatever power is at their disposal to build their own empire, no matter what the cost for others. This is true in the worlds of politics, of finance, of education, of social standing, and of religion. There have always been people— and I fear there will be until God's kingdom comes—who do not care what happens to others, particularly those who compete with them, if only they can get their way. Whether they acknowledge it or not, they intend harm for those who get in their way. But God intends good.

So it is that good keeps rising up, no matter how strong the odds are for evil. These stories come one upon another in the history of nations and in the stories of individual lives and daily human relationships. The stories number in the billions: every moment, in some corner of the world or another, someone intends harm to another, but God turns the evil toward good.

I am reassured and strengthened by this knowledge and by the faith that flows from it. Paul states in Romans 8:28: "We know that all things work together for good for those who love God, who are called according to his purpose." The key phrase, it seems to me, is *"according to his purpose."* If God has a purpose for our universe, then our individual lives have a purpose, to the extent that we are willing to give them to the purposes of God. When our lives are affiliated with the purposes of God, there is a providential guarantee of right fortune.

So an exciting prospect lies before us. The universe in which we live is not a chaos without meaning, and it is not unfolding helter-skelter. Any given day or series of events may be quite disorderly; if we view these days and events without faith, we may conclude that if a discernible pattern ever emerges, it will be either a miracle or a product of utter chance. But the apostle Paul was sure that God has a purpose, and that God's love is so dominant and God's intelligence so encompassing that *all things* are working together for good. This includes not only the good that you and I may earnestly contribute to the mix; it includes also all the irrational, mean, destructive, and buffoonish things we humans throw into the story. God's interest in us and in our universe is such that out of evil's ugliness can emerge the beauty of God's ultimate purpose.

This principle operates both at an intimate, personal level and within the history of nations and of movements, as the story of Joseph demonstrates and as Joseph himself testified. His brothers intended evil, but only toward their brother (though they recognized the pain their father would experience—pain that perhaps they felt he deserved because of his favoritism toward Joseph). As Joseph interpreted the events, God was using the events for good, not only in Joseph's preservation and elevation to a position of power (matters to which Joseph made no reference, in fact). What impressed Joseph was that God's intention was "to preserve a numerous people, as he is doing today." Joseph was the particular instrument of this good, but he saw himself as incidental to the story. God was unfolding purposes for nations, and for centuries to come, and God was doing so in spite of human evil. Indeed, God was actually using human evil for good.

Consider what happened generations later, with Moses. The nation of Israel had been in bondage for centuries, long enough for any conception of freedom or of human dignity to be lost. Somehow, however, it remained, like smoldering coals from a long-ago fire. By providence a son of slaves was raised in a royal palace. With all those comfortable advantages, Moses managed somehow to keep a sense of his ethnic heritage and with it a sense of justice, so that one day, when he "saw an Egyptian beating a Hebrew, one of his kinsfolk," he killed the Egyptian (Exod. 2:11–12).

Violent as it was, Moses's act was idealistic; he wanted justice. Instead, the murder made Moses a fugitive. If you and I had been observing all of this from a box seat, we would have built up hope in Moses's upbringing in the palace and in his awakening social conscience as a man of forty. Then our hopes would have been destroyed by Moses's misuse of his sense of justice and by his subsequent banishment to a Midian desert. It would have been hard to believe that years in that desert would prepare Moses to become his people's deliverer and history's premier lawgiver.

Can good come out of evil? It happens by the hour, by the moment, ten thousands of times a day around the world. It is God's major enterprise in our world. The book of Genesis tells us that when God created the heavens and the earth, "the earth was a formless void and darkness covered the face of the deep" (Gen. 1:2). That scene seems like an appropriate beginning for all that has ensued. Ever since, God has been dealing with the formlessness, the void, and the darkness that so much of our human conduct inflicts upon this planet. God has been redeeming this darkness and shaping the formlessness with purpose. This is so on a much smaller scale, with the routine pain of life. John Wesley looked at Jesus' words, "So do not worry about tomorrow, for tomorrow will bring worries of its own" (Matt. 6:34), and commented, "but all trouble is, upon the whole, a real good."[4] I think Wesley was realistic enough to acknowledge that most of us bring a good share of our troubles upon ourselves. Nevertheless, God seems dedicated to bringing good out of even our own unwitting acts of self-destruction—yes, even some of our deliberate acts, because often enough we are our own worst enemies, our own worst impediment to the will of God operating in our lives.

God works too through the evil others inflict upon us. Kathleen Norris tells of a Benedictine monk who—years after the occurrences—began to recognize that when he was a teenager he had been sexually abused by a priest. "Over time," Ms. Norris writes, "his dreadful pain over the irretrievable loss of innocence began to be converted into a blessing for other people." She goes on to observe that while "the lid closes on what went before," we can't deny the past. "All the baggage comes along; nothing wasted, nothing lost. Perhaps the greatest blessing that religious inheritance can bestow is an open mind, one that can listen without judging."[5]

As I look back on my own life, I thank God daily for those persons whose wisdom and love blessed me and to whom I owe so much today. I also recall persons who have hurt me. Some of them intended to do so. As I look at myself, I think they may have had reason to feel as they did—not always, but sometimes. Others laid burdens on me unintentionally, not because they were mean but because they were human, and thus at times inept. One should not dwell unduly upon the past, but one should look at it long enough and with enough intelligence and forgiveness to make use of it. As Ms. Norris has said, let all the baggage come along, "nothing wasted, nothing lost."

God can always transform life's paraphernalia into purpose. The pain we have experienced, whether by sickness or human tragedy or by the intentional or unintentional acts of others, can become a blessing in the process of our own growth and a blessing we can extend to others. It is up to us to accept these unlikely stones and to make of them building blocks of a worthy life edifice. God wills it to be so, because God is on the side of goodness. It is up to us, however, to decide whether we want to cooperate with God and goodness, or whether we will choose to retreat into a cave of self-pity or recrimination and resentment.

Joseph's story indicates a remarkable readiness to use his fortunes and misfortunes for good. As a slave in the house of Potiphar, he worked so industriously that he became the most trusted member of the household. When his integrity cost him his position, he set about using his life in prison as faithfully as he had used it in slavery. When the cupbearer to the king forgot Joseph for two years, Joseph did not allow his gifts to die in disappointment and futility; when the call came from Pharaoh's court, Joseph's skills were clearly ready for immediate employment. No wonder, then, that when his brothers appealed to him for mercy many years later, Joseph could look back on all of his life and say, "God meant it for good." While he was speaking particularly of and to his brothers, he could have included in his evaluation Potiphar's wife, a forgetful steward, and only God knows how many other passing incidents and persons. God's purpose was not frustrated by human sin or human error. The only thing that could have frustrated God's purpose in Joseph's life would have been a failure on Joseph's part to cooperate with the purposes of God. Mind you, the ultimate purposes of God would not have been stopped, but if Joseph had not cooperated, the unfolding of God's will might have been delayed (as I am sure it has been, repeatedly, in human history and in our personal lives), and someone other than Joseph might have become God's instrument.

Naturally most of us are concerned about the will and purposes of God as they show themselves in our own daily lives—in our careers, our human relationships, our general faith journey, and our physical health. J. B. Phillips, the Anglican rector who blessed the English-speaking world just after World War II with his translation of the New Testament, believed in the possibility of physical healing through prayer. But he pondered also the peculiar way sickness sometimes works in our lives. "I am sure," he wrote, "that disease is in itself evil, but I am left wondering how the courage, love and compassion it evokes would be produced in a world where everybody was perfectly healthy."[6]

It is a question worth thinking about. Disease is itself evil; it is not the ideal for the kingdom of God. But I venture that every one of us can point to good that has come as a result of sickness. One of the loveliest believers I have known is grateful for her multiple sclerosis because of what it has done for her walk with God and her general pattern of character. She does not want to return to the kind of person she was before the affliction began its inroads on her body.

I think too of a colleague in Florida, a good and godly man who for the past several years has watched over the body of his adult daughter, who was infected by a mosquito bite that has left her in a deteriorating coma. He assures me that he has learned a great deal about himself and about faith and has become a better person through his daughter's tragic illness. Mind you, the illness *is* tragic—for the diminution (at least as we know it) of the daughter's life, as well as the emotional pain that her parents and friends continue to suffer. God did not cause her illness. And yet, God—with the cooperation of a believing father—is bringing a measure of good out of the evil that she and her family have suffered.

At this point I want to be very clear about two matters. First, I disagree vehemently with those who would say that God sent the multiple sclerosis on my friend or that it was God's will for the disease-laden mosquito to infect my friend's daughter. God does not bring about evil in order to demonstrate superior power; this is a monstrous thought. In truth, there is no need for *God* to send evil. We humans do quite well on our own. If we would eliminate all the tragedies caused by human greed, we would be well on our way to a more perfect world. I accept the fact that there are always "Joseph's brothers" in our world (aided often by misguided "fathers" who provoke the brothers) to provide pain and problems, and I see no reason to put God in the equation until we allow God to come in, by our readiness to cooperate with God's purposes.

We should not worry too much about why God does not intervene in all of our complicated doings. As J. B. Phillips has reminded us, we cannot have such intervention without interfering with the gift of personal choice. In the instances of pain caused by illness or natural disaster, I will direct my energy to help alleviate such pain: by prayer always, by financial or physical support where such can be given, and by supporting the suffering person by any means within my reach.

In truth, I no longer spend much time wondering why evil happens. Most of it is explainable in our human conduct, and for that which is beyond my understanding I have decided to put my energy instead into cooperating with redemption. I marvel unceasingly at God's redemption at work every day, everywhere. With J. B. Phillips I affirm that the ultimate purposes of God can never be defeated.

But I do fear that the purposes of God can be delayed if we human beings fail to cooperate with God. We cannot remain inert and expect God's will to happen. I wonder what would happen if all of us who pray the Lord's Prayer—*"thy kingdom come, thy will be done, on earth as it is in heaven"*—were to live that prayer? What if all of us kingdom people lived out our prayers, from the way we respond to the person at the checkout counter, to the way we function in Congress, to the skills we bring to the laboratories and classrooms?

I know full well that there is evil in the world. I have seen it in a variety of human forms and in forms of disease and disaster beyond my understanding. But I have also seen—and marveled at—the way good comes out of evil. Every day I shake my head in holy astonishment at this unfolding mystery that persons—or something malevolent in the universe—mean deeds for evil, but God turns them for good.

And then I marvel at our potential role in all of this mystery.

Chapter 5

JESUS AND THE WILL OF GOD

What can we learn from Jesus about the will of God? For those of us who call ourselves Christians, any discussion of the will of God needs to place Jesus at the center of the discussion, early and continually. If Jesus is our Lord, our teacher, and our example, we want to know how he understood the will of God and how he tried to live it out in his own life. As a matter of fact, millions of people who don't identify themselves as Christians, but who nevertheless revere Jesus as the best example of humanity, clearly care more about what Jesus himself said concerning the will of God than they do about the insights of accumulated philosophers and theologians. So what of Jesus and the will of God?

Perhaps there is no better place to begin than with the prayer Jesus gave us, commonly known as the Lord's Prayer. It is fair to say that this prayer is probably the most widely used expression of devotion among Christians on our planet. Unfortunately, our familiarity often frustrates our thoughtful consideration of what the prayer says. It is difficult to give proper weight to the words in this prayer, not only because we know them so well, but also because we are misled by what seems to be their artless simplicity. In truth it is this very simplicity that lays such strategic demands on us.

This brief prayer—only fifty to seventy words in the various English translations—includes a petition that the will of God be done in our world. This petition about God's will is the first of the four petitions in the prayer. Even before our prayer for daily bread, before the cry for the forgiveness of our sins, and before our plea to be protected from evil, comes this key petition:

> Your kingdom come,
> Your will be done,
>   on earth as it is in heaven.
>   Matt. 6:10

Of course this emphasis should not really surprise us. Jesus began his ministry by announcing that the kingdom of heaven had come near, "the good news of the kingdom" (Matt. 4:17, 23), and much of his Sermon on the Mount (found in Matt. 5–7) is a description of the quality of life that will mark this kingdom. No wonder, then, that a petition for God's kingdom would lead the way in the prayer Jesus gave us as our model. Whatever else we pray for each day, whatever else we seek to bring to pass, this is the beginning: that God's will be done, on earth as it is in heaven.

Much could be said about this simple, forthright petition, but two things in particular must be highlighted. First, the will of God will not be done simply because God wills that it shall be so. If the will of God is going to be done, no matter what we do or say or pray, then Jesus' prayer is a charade, an exercise in divine playfulness. Why pray for something to happen if it is already certain to happen? If the will of God were a guaranteed happening, the prayer might then rightly offer thanks to God for the assurance that his will would be done, or it might express our rejoicing in the confidence we feel regarding the divine will. But this is not the form Jesus employed. He chose instead to pray that God's "will be done, on earth as in heaven," and he encouraged his disciples to do the same. Jesus was telling his followers to pray for something that God wanted to see happen, the divine will.

Second, this phrase in our kingdom prayer indicates that prayer is a factor in bringing God's will to pass. I will deal with this thought more fully later.

Let us look at an instance where Jesus contemplated the kind of question that so often comes up in our present-day discussions about the will of God, the kind of enigma that intrigues our sense of fairness in the events that occur in the world. The Gospel of Luke tells the story of a group of Galilean pilgrims who had come to Jerusalem to worship but had been brutally murdered by Pilate's soldiers, so that their blood was mixed with the blood of the sacrifices they had brought with them (Luke 13:1). It was an incident with the kind of emotional impact one feels when a couple is tragically killed on their honeymoon, or when young people on a mission service trip are killed in a bus accident. Apparently the Galilean incident was being widely discussed at the time, particularly for its theological significance. Why had these people been so victimized? Was it because they had sinned, so that their death was God's judgment?

Jesus rebuked such thinking: "Do you think that because these Galileans suffered in this way they were worse sinners than all other Galileans? No, I tell you; but unless you repent, you will all perish as they did" (Luke 13:2–3). Jesus continued by referring to a similar sort of inexplicable tragedy, when eighteen people were killed when the tower in Siloam fell on them (Luke 13:4). Again Jesus said, "Do you think that they were worse offenders than all the others living in Jerusalem?" Again Jesus rejected the idea that these persons were selected victims of judgment (Luke 13:5).

It is quite astonishing that the questions Jesus dealt with on that occasion continue to reappear generation after generation, among people of almost every degree of religious persuasion. We want to find some logic in the tragedies that occur. In the instances to which Jesus referred, the origin of the problem might have been seen in the actions of a tyrannical ruler or a failure in the building code or the work of the masons. But somehow we are not willing to settle the matter at such obvious levels. Instead, we are plagued by the "Why" question. Why does this community suffer the tornado and the next town escape? Why was my friend killed by a drunken driver, rather than the person who was with him? Because there is a surprising moralistic streak in even the most religiously indifferent, someone will quickly find an answer: it is judgment upon sinful conduct.

Jesus rejected any such quid pro quo reasoning. If you think these tragedies are God's judgments on sin, Jesus answered, then watch out, because "unless you repent, you will all perish just as they did" (Luke 13:5). None of us are perfect. The fact that we have escaped peril should not give us a feeling of self-satisfaction. Things happen, and they cannot always—perhaps in fact can only rarely—be explained as judgments of God. It might not be irreverent of me to imagine a further word from Jesus: Just be grateful that you were not at the tower of Siloam that day.

If you or someone you love has met with inexplicable tragedy, I believe Jesus would tell you, as he told that crowd so long ago: "This is not the judgment of God." If you escaped such a possible tragedy ("Do you know, we originally planned to go to Siloam that day, but our trip was delayed!"), it is appropriate for you to be thankful and feel moved to live more circumspectly, out of gratitude for a life or a limb spared. But I would not conclude that God loved you more than those who died or were injured in the tragedy. Nor would I endorse your testimony if you reported that God spared you but let the others be hurt. As Jesus said, we are all deserving of judgment, and when the events of this life unfold in their inexplicable way, we should not try either to blame God or to praise God for what happened. Be grateful if you are a survivor, and pray for grace if you or someone you love is a victim; but do not think of God as manipulating the world according to your prescription.

As for his own life, Jesus saw the will of God as the compelling element of who he was and of what he did. Consider the day in Samaria when Jesus had his visit with the woman at the well. When his disciples returned from the city with food, they urged, "Rabbi, eat something." Jesus replied, "I have food to eat that you do not know about." As was so often the case—especially as reported in John's Gospel—the disciples were very literalistic; thus they said to one another, "Surely no one has brought him something to eat?" Jesus answered, "My food is to do the will of him who sent me and to complete his work" (John 4:31–34). Jesus found his very sustenance in fulfilling the will of God in his life.

Jesus spoke in the same fashion to those who wanted to put an end to his ministry. When they challenged his healing on the Sabbath, Jesus replied, "I can do nothing on my own. As I hear, I judge; and my judgment is just, because I seek to do not my own will, but the will of him who sent me" (John 5:30). He saw his life as having two possible choices, to do his own will or to do the will of God, the one who had sent him. The right course of action was thus very simple: Do what God had sent him to do. Do the will and purpose of the one who had commissioned him.

Jesus became even more emphatic when some pressed him for a sign of his authority. "I have come down from heaven," Jesus said, "not to do my own will, but the will of him who sent me" (John 6:38). He dared to allude to his divinity ("I have come down from heaven"—a phrase that offended his listeners) but put himself under complete submission to his assignment to do the will of the one who had sent him.

The unknown author of the book of Hebrews picked up the same theme dramatically when he explained how Christ's death superceded the Old Testament pattern of blood sacrifices: "Consequently, when Christ came into the world, he said, 'Sacrifices and offerings you have not desired, but a body you have prepared for me; in burnt offerings and sin offerings you have taken no pleasure. Then I said, "See, God, I have come to do your will, O God"'" (Heb. 10:5–7). In this instance the writer of Hebrews drew from Psalm 40:6–7. In doing so, he underlined the understanding of the earliest Christians that not only had Jesus come from God as the Christ, but that his singular purpose in doing so was to do the will of God. The matter is so crucial that the writer repeats it a few words later: "then he [Jesus] added, 'See, I have come to do your will'" (Heb. 10:9).

We might therefore rightly say that this is what Christmas is all about: that Jesus came into our world to bring the will of God to pass. We could very well call Christmas the "Will of God Day," because Christmas celebrates God's action, through Christ, of bringing the will of God into our world.

This brings us to the crucial hour in the crucial weekend of our Lord's passion, death, and resurrection. Jesus and his disciples had eaten together in an upper room, celebrating the Passover, which Jesus then took to another level as he gave the disciples the bread and the cup and told them that they were eating of his body and blood. They then sang a hymn and went on to the Mount of Olives (Matt. 26:26–30). As they went, Jesus warned them that all of them would "become deserters." Peter immediately denied any such possibility, even to the point of putting down his fellow disciples: "Though all become deserters . . . I will never desert you." Jesus answered that in fact Peter would deny him three times before the cock crowed twice, which inspired Peter to insist vehemently, "Even though I must die with you, I will not deny you." All of his colleagues said the same (Matt. 26:31–35).

By this time they had reached the garden called Gethsemane, and Jesus went alone to pray. At this point Jesus entered the "Calvary before Calvary." He began now to comprehend what Calvary would be like. Jesus said, "I am deeply grieved, even to death; remain here, and stay awake with me" (Matt. 26:38). *Even to death.* Jesus was moving into the realm of death itself. Particularly, as I see it, he was moving into the time when he would feel the absence of his Father's love. This would be a death beyond death. Death takes the life of the body; what Jesus was about to experience was death to his very soul, as he felt himself cut off from God.

If we lose the sense of God's character—God's justice, love, grace, and mercy—we have lost God. At the cross Jesus would cry out, "My God, why have you forsaken me?" (Matt. 27:46). This quality of forsakenness began in Gethsemane. Jesus knew there the desolation of soul that lay ahead. Luke declares that Jesus' anguish in prayer was so great that "his sweat became like great drops of blood falling down on the ground" (Luke 22:44).

What was the issue that caused such agony of prayer and such an expectation of total abandonment? Jesus was confronting the issue of the will of God in his own life. This was the will that had governed and directed his conduct and thinking from the day he confronted hell in the wilderness of temptation—and indeed, no doubt long before that. Jesus had said that his food was to do the will of the one who had sent him. He had told his antagonists that he had come down from heaven, not to do his own will, but the will of the one who sent him. But now, seeing the consequences of that will up close, only hours away, Jesus made a searching prayer. "Abba, Father, for you all things are possible; remove this cup from me; yet, not what I want, but what you want"—or in the familiar cadences of the King James Version, "Nevertheless not what I will, but what thou wilt" (Mark 14:36).

Since God has a will for our planet, and since there is something on our planet—and something too often expressed in our human conduct—that opposes this will, it is obvious that God's will has a price. When we dedicate ourselves to God's will, we enter conflict against all that is opposed to God's will.

For Jesus, being true to God's will meant being abandoned by his followers. They were not evil men. I will not even accuse them, as we often do, of being weak men. They simply could not comprehend the cost involved in doing God's will. In this, they were like most of us. The disciples found it easy to imagine Christ in his kingdom, with them ruling at his right and left, but they could not imagine the struggle to bring in the kingdom. When Jesus went to Gethsemane to pray, he asked the best of his team, Peter, James, and John, to watch with him, though at a distance. But they fell asleep (Mark 14:32–42). The Gospel writers tell us that they were weary, as indeed they were, but I suspect that their falling asleep is also symbolic. They were simply dull to the issues involved in the will of God: "Your kingdom come, your will be done." The kingdom of God's will comes not through our relaxation but through our disciplined commitment.

Jesus' prayer is instructive. The Scriptures make clear that our Lord was fully human in his brief years on earth. In that humanness he asked, as all of us do, if we can achieve God's will without its enormous price, because we achieve the will of God by forfeiting our own will or, more specifically, by submitting our will to the will of God. Most of the time, this act of submission is not all that dramatic or painful, though of course we may see it differently at the time. Many of us realize later that what we once thought was our Gethsemane was only a rather ordinary garden path. No matter; our perceptions define reality at the time of their unfolding, and we are not fair to ourselves when we redefine those perceptions later with the benefit of hindsight.

Nevertheless, it is unfortunate to look upon each decision as a kind of Gethsemane or Calvary. G. A. Studdert-Kennedy knew a very great deal about the struggle with evil during his years as a chaplain in World War I and in his ministry at a city parish in London following the war. He insisted that we should see in Jesus' prayer not so much submission as an act of positive and powerful aspiration.[1] To want God's will to be done is, for sure, a submitting of our own will to the will of God. But this is a grand act of conquest, not of defeat.

See, then, how Jesus left Gethsemane. "The hour has come; the Son of Man is betrayed into the hands of sinners. Get up, let us be going. See, my betrayer is at hand" (Mark 14:41–42). Our Lord was as matter of fact as the coal miner who picks up his lunch bucket to enter another day's work in the bowels of the earth. It was his assignment, the very purpose for which he had come into the world—to do the will of his Father in heaven. It would not be easy. Who could expect the kingdom to come with ease, when all the wisdom of hell and all the foolishness of earth were pitted against it?

It *will* be victorious. The kingdom of God—God's ultimate will for this universe—will be done. Jesus settled that matter once and for all when he walked from Gethsemane. And he says to us, as he said to his disciples then, "Get up, let us be going" (Mark 14:42).

Chapter 6

THE WILL OF GOD
AND PRAYER

Almost everyone believes in prayer, in one form or another
and to some degree or another. I am quite sure that in times
of stress many professed atheists pray, but then feel guilty
for having done so.

Prayer is probably never more universal than in
times of major natural disasters or at the peaks of war activity. In such times of trial and disaster the prayers get inter-
twined with the issues of the will of God. In one breath the
person asks, "How do you explain a thing like this?" then
answers as if it were a rhetorical question, "It must have
been the will of God," and the conversational companion
replies, "At times like these there isn't much any of us can
do except pray."

If someone were to ask, "Pray for what?" the other
party might find it hard to answer. Some mean to pray for
understanding, so they will know how to cope with the
inexplicable and the frightening. Others mean that we
should pray for the victims, that relief may come or that
they will get the strength to deal with their losses, however severe those losses may be. Still others are thinking
of a miracle and pray for something wonderful to happen,
so that the worst of the tragedy can somehow be averted
or turned into surprising gain. All seem to agree, however, that at such a time prayer is not only an appropriate

response, but is in fact the most appropriate response, the only really logical thing to do.

If a tragedy has already occurred, this counsel, for any of the reasons mentioned, seems altogether right. To pray for understanding is both the least of prayers and the best of prayers: the least because it calls for divine intervention at a level where our own cooperation can play the largest part in bringing an answer to our prayer, and the best because such understanding involves a quality of truly godly character. To pray for the victims is humane and loving, and certainly we should do this kind of praying. One can hardly imagine a sensitive person who isn't moved to prayer by the grief of another. But this kind of prayer can also be an easy way out, when perhaps we should be putting legs to our prayers by contributing money to relieve the victims' distress or joining some rebuilding operation. As for praying for a miracle, we must acknowledge that some don't believe in prayer at that level. It is also true, however—even if not particularly logical—that some who pray only rarely are among those who will pray most unashamedly for the altogether miraculous.

All of these prayers involve a prior question: Does God care about what happens in our world? Is God unconscious of what happens on our planet, detached from both its joys and sorrows? As I read the Scriptures and as I look at the lives of those we call saints (persons who know God best), the answer is nearly unanimous: God does indeed care about what happens in our world, and God is altogether conscious of our concerns. The most vigorous questioning of God in the Scriptures comes from those persons who at some point of trial are tempted to believe otherwise and who argue with both God and themselves that God must be better than the doubts they are entertaining. God cares, and we are strengthened in our time of struggle by the knowledge of God's caring.

Of course there is another prior question, which also involves God's involvement in our world but portrays God in a quite different way. What if one believes, as many profess to do, that everything which happens in our world is according to the will of God? I'm thinking of those who say in the midst of tragedy, "It must have been the will of God." A person with such convictions is able to pray, and to pray well, for those who are suffering. But if our prayer begins with the assumption that "whatever will be, will be," then our prayers will be limited to a petition for God to sustain through trials and to give strength for the times of suffering. If whatever happens in our world is the will of God, then any prayer for the will of God to be done is after the fact. There is no reason to pray for the will of God to be done, but only that we will be able to endure or to cope with what happens, since whatever happens is the will of God and is therefore inevitable.

I do not believe that everything which happens in our world is God's will. The Scriptures teach that our prayers play a part in bringing the will of God to pass. Thus, if we neglect to pray or stop praying, we allow the will of God to be delayed. I believe that the larger, ultimate purposes of God will eventually happen and that God's kingdom will indeed someday come. But *when* the purposes of God are fulfilled—and perhaps also *how* they come to pass—depends on both our deeds and our prayers. Much of the anguish that our world suffers could be avoided if we prayed and if we prayed more earnestly and unceasingly. There are no neutral parties in this struggle between good and evil in our world. You and I are lending our strength to either good or evil. We cannot assume a position of neutrality in this unceasing battle.

All of us who are in any way influenced by the Scriptures of the Old and New Testaments believe we cannot be neutral in matters of our daily conduct. If a loved one is ill, we seek medical help; we don't stand idly by and say, "It is God's will to decide if he will live or die; therefore I won't interfere." Nor will anyone in his or her right mind refuse relief from suffering. It is unthinkable to imagine standing by while someone suffers, arguing, "If God wants her to suffer, who am I to interfere with the will of God?" No one who can swim will watch someone drown while reasoning that the person's survival is up to the will of God. Rather, we feel compelled to lend our strength and skill to saving the life.

Ironically, we sometimes hesitate to pray the way we act. When I was a pastor, I dealt more than once with earnest, troubled people who said, as a loved one faced some major medical crisis, "I don't really know how I should pray. Do I have a right to pray for him/her to be healed?" My answer was pragmatic. If one is really uncertain about whether the person should be well, one is putting quite a moral burden on the physicians and the hospital staff, because, in seeking to preserve that person's life, they may be opposing God.

Of course there does indeed come a time to die, and because of the wonderful advances in medical science that have developed almost exponentially in the past fifty years, we humans now play a much larger part in determining when death finally takes control. Do we then conclude that it is God's will for this person to live, because they happen to be within reach of a medical center that specializes in their type of illness, and that it is God's will for the person in the less advantageous position to die? Do we conclude that it is God's will for infants to die in shocking numbers in some parts of the world, while in others God is pleased that more infants live? I think not. If we have a biblical picture of God, we feel compelled to bring to as many persons as possible as many health benefits as possible. In doing so, we are cooperating with the will of God.

So is God involved in these matters? Does God care about matters of life and death, suffering and relief? If so, where does prayer come in? Indeed, does prayer matter? Or is everything, rather, a matter of location and economic benefits—living in areas where medical care is expert, or being so fortunate as to have a wise and an especially attentive family physician? Is it God's will for the child of the economically advantaged parents to live, and for the child of the ghetto family to die? Is God's will tilted in favor of those who have better health insurance? Where, if at all, does prayer play a part?

Consider again the prayer our Lord taught us. In it we *pray* for God's will to be done—as in heaven, so on earth. We don't assume that the will of God will be done regardless of our prayers, nor do we assume that our works of righteousness are enough to bring the will of God to pass and that thus there is no need to support these works by our prayers. As I have said earlier, if God's will is going to be done regardless of our work or our prayers, then Jesus was playing games with his followers when he instructed us to pray for God's will to be done and for God's kingdom to come.

Further, Jesus gave us a pattern of expectation. We pray for earth to become like heaven. The will of God is done in heaven; with that pattern in mind, we pray for God's will to be done on earth. Believers live in a wonderful tension between gratitude for what is and discontent with its not being enough. We thank God for each small gain in holiness, purity, health, or justice, and we press for more, since we still are not enjoying the pattern of heaven. In the language of Charles Wesley, "What shall I do to thank my God for all His mercy's store? / I'll take the gifts He hath bestowed and humbly ask for more."[1]

"Thy will be done." This is both the most frightening and the most reassuring of all prayers. It's frightening because if we mean it, we are giving up control. We are telling God that we believe the divine will for our world and for our lives is better than our own will. To pray this prayer is to sign a blank check and to trust God to write in the particulars. This is also the most reassuring and the safest of all prayers. What could be safer than the will of a gracious, all-knowing God? How could we be better off than to put all our affairs, including our future, into the hands of such a Lord? Nevertheless, it is an act of faith, and as such it is a frightening leap.

We can speak with certainty about the ultimate will of God. Jesus gave us a definition: "as it is in heaven." It is presumptuous to become unduly specific about God's will. Without hesitancy I say that the will of God—for our world, for our generation, for you and for me—is *good.* But I know better than to define *good*—for our world, for our generation, for you or me. Since ours is not a perfect world, the road that leads to God's will is likely to be marked by a variety of detours and construction. Are those hard places the will of God? Not really, but because of the nature of our world they are places to be passed through in gaining the perfect will of God.

When I begin, however, to pray for a specific need or concern, I begin with assumptions about the good. I assume that life is better than death, health is better than sickness, fullness is better than poverty, love is better than hate. Several years ago a cherished friend was dealing with a painful illness that was bringing him to the edge of death. I asked God, apologetically, that if my friend was to die, he might die in comfort. Then I caught myself. This was no matter for apology. From all I know of God, God wants the best for us humans. To pray for my friend to be free of pain was just the way I ought to pray; it was a prayer that reinforced the purposes of God.

Pain often draws us closer to God, and many a person in pain has later testified to the eternal value of the pain they endured, but when I pray, I have to go with what I know. I know that God's ultimate will for us is *good*. Ordinarily pain and suffering are not good, though God surely can and does bring good out of them on numerous occasions. So I will pray for what, in my human limitations, I know—and I will trust God to handle my prayer with divine wisdom. That is, I will trust God to hear the *intent* of my prayer rather than the faulty language of my human knowledge.

The apostle Paul gave us an interesting example in his own struggle with a problem and an unanswered prayer. He confided that he had become elated over some of his spiritual experiences and that "a thorn was given me in the flesh, a messenger of Satan to torment me." Three times he prayed to be delivered from this torment, but the Lord replied, "My grace is sufficient for you, for power is made perfect in weakness." Paul continues that he was therefore accepting this weakness "all the more gladly" because of the power it brought to his ministry (2 Cor. 12:7–10). Paul had felt justified in seeking relief from his affliction (whatever it was; scholars offer wide-ranging possibilities) until God made clear to him that this burden was part of God's purpose in his life. So I believe that we should pray for what seems to be a reasonable request—and continue praying, it seems to me, unless one is deeply impressed that God has a purpose in the request being refused.

Why should we pray for the will of God? If something is God's will, will it not come to pass without our prayers? If it is God's will, does God need our help or a reminder from us to bring about what is already the divine intention?

When we pray, several things happen. For one, our own sensitivity is heightened. We may see how we can contribute to a solution, or we may come to a better, more thoughtful understanding. These changes within the person who is praying may well play a part in bringing an answer to our prayers.

But I believe still more is involved. When we pray, we become agents in bringing the will of God to pass. There is much in our world that is opposed to the will of God, some of it obvious and very human and some of it probably quite beyond our full comprehension. If a flood wall breaks in the midst of a natural disaster, we may wonder what part politics, economics, and human inertia played in settling for an inadequate wall. When a disease or an infection takes someone's life, we may wonder if an overworked and weary nurse, a hasty and inadequate cleansing of a worker's hands, or a physician going beyond his knowledge contributed to the death. So many factors in our world can thwart the immediate will of God, and so many of them are in some measure spiritual—indifference, emotional and physical weariness, preoccupation, irritation, willful ignorance. The list is quite endless.

In the midst of such opposition to what is best, the believer ought to pray for the will of God to be done. To do so is not to twist the divine arm, but to cooperate with the divine purpose. Walter Brueggemann, the eminent Old

Testament scholar, reminds us of the words of Karl Barth: "God is not deaf, but listens; more than that, he acts. God does not act in the same way whether we pray or not. Prayer exerts an influence upon God's action, even upon his existence. This is what the word 'answer' means."[2]

Jesus saw this as part of the principle of prayer. When he appointed seventy persons to go "to every town and place where he himself intended to go" (Luke 10:1), he noted that the harvest was all out of proportion to the few laborers he was sending out. Our logic begins thinking of a program to enlist more workers or to seek to deploy our present staff more wisely. But listen to Jesus' counsel: "Ask the Lord of the harvest to send out laborers into his harvest" (Luke 10:2). Why ask God to send out laborers when God already knows that laborers are needed? Why ask God to do what clearly is God's will? Because by our prayers—as by our labors—we cooperate with God in bringing God's will to pass.

The apostle Paul employed the same principle in his appeal to the church at Rome. He asked the people to join "in earnest prayer to God on my behalf," that he might be rescued from unbelievers who put his ministry in peril, and "so that *by God's will* I may come to you with joy and be refreshed in your company" (Rom. 15:30–32; emphasis added). Everything Paul wanted was proper, indeed was the will of God, but Paul was pleading with the people to pray for it to happen. Whatever the purposes of God in our world, God has left the implementation in our hands. One of the instruments of that implementation is prayer.

No wonder, then, that Paul instructed his followers to pray without ceasing (1 Thess. 5:17). There is opposition to the will of God in our world. If we cease to pray, we forfeit the battle. When we use the phrase "May the will

of God be done," we are inclined to use it in a tone of res-
ignation, almost as if we are expecting the worst, when in
truth this phrase ought to be seen as a shout of triumph, a
declaration thrust into the teeth of hell. Charles J. Chaput,
archbishop of Denver, quotes Karl Barth: "To clasp the
hands in prayer is the beginning of an uprising against the
disorder of the world."[3]

When we pray for the will of God, we are joining
hands with God to bring God's will to pass in our world.
Prayer is an instrument for the will of God as surely as are
godly living, godly serving, and dedicated resistance to all
that is evil. We are never more in tune with God than when,
in commitment and holy excitement, we pray, "Your will
be done, as in heaven, so on earth."

Chapter 7

COOPERATING
WITH THE WILL OF GOD

Among the true twentieth-century giants of faith, few stand higher than Frank Laubach. Many honor him as a great missionary for his early service in the Philippines. Millions more know him as a genius in his understanding of prayer, a person who could translate Christian mysticism into a "game with minutes."[1] But far more—an uncounted number—have been Laubach's beneficiaries because through him (though they may not know his name) they have learned to read. His "each one teach one" program now has numerous mutations around the world, but they spring from Laubach's application of the principle of personal evangelism in the field of literacy.

What made Frank Laubach run? He had extraordinary gifts, but untold thousands of gifted people make little impact on our world. I submit that a crucial secret in this man's life can be found in the prayer with which he began each day: "God, what are you doing in the world today that I can help you with?"

I am convinced beyond doubt that God is at work in our world. God has more at stake in this universe than even the most committed of us. Since this is so, the ultimate issue for you and me is to see where God is at work—that is, where God's will is evident—and to join God in that enterprise.

The will of God is a cooperative enterprise. Our world cannot ultimately thwart it, because it is in the purpose of God. As I have indicated elsewhere, we can delay God's will, we can make it less accessible, and we can make our world more miserable by getting in the way of this will. But because it is the will of God, it will come in time.

God chooses not to have it without our cooperation. God may have to wait very long to see the kingdom come. Many skirmishes between good and evil may for a time be posted as victories for evil, but eventually the will of God will be accomplished, as you and I and the generations following us cooperate with God's purposes. It seems evident that God is willing to wait. Clearly, so much rests on us humans. Thus Jesus finished one of his parables on prayer by asking, "When the Son of Man comes, will he find faith on earth?" (Luke 18:8). This is the question with which you and I must deal whenever we ponder the will of God in our world.

There is work to be done. The morning news, whether delivered by newspaper, radio, television, or Internet, shows how much waits to be done. At the same time, the better side of the news tells us that much *is* being done, a fact that ought to encourage us each day as we set out to take our place in the fields of human need. If we are committed to cooperating in God's will, we ought to be invigorated by the knowledge that God is with us in our efforts and that therefore ultimate victory is assured.

Unfortunately, much of the time we conduct our lives as if God's will were no issue, and as if we have no part in seeing God's will come to pass. We fail to involve ourselves because of the common assumptions with which we live so much of our lives, assumptions summarized in phrases of our common beliefs. When we speak these phrases, we hardly realize that we are enunciating our theology. It almost never occurs to us that these common phrases may influence the way we live our lives.

Think, for instance, of the phrase that is often spoken in the face of hardship or tragedy: "Well, everything happens for a reason." Not really. Everything happens as the result of some cause, but whether there is a reason—whether anything purposeful will come from it—is up to us. God has a reason, a goal for our lives and our creation, but the extent and timing of that reason is up to us. You and I have to make the reason happen. With God's help, we must bring purpose out of the chaos of circumstances. We must cooperate in bringing God's will to pass.

"Everything happens for a reason" and other phrases like it can easily become a holy cop-out. The person speaking this phrase generally means it to be an expression of faith, as if all that happens is part of God's plan. Of course, if this is so, then there is nothing that we either can or ought to do.

Perhaps the reason that continuing generations have said, "Everything happens for a reason," is that in every generation a few persons have concluded just the opposite and have set out to bring good out of what was manifestly not good. They have sought to do something about the problems and the tragedies and heartbreak they met, and through their efforts a "reason" has indeed developed. But it didn't happen willy-nilly. It happened because someone's efforts brought purpose out of problems. Because of the efforts and the prayers of people who refuse to make peace with things as they are, others can go on believing and trusting that eventually things work out all right. Under God we can dare to become part of the solutions rather than acquiescing to the problems.

In 2005 the tragedy named Hurricane Katrina inspired many people to react with faith and with the action that springs from faith. When United Methodist Bishop Hope Morgan Ward was asked to describe what was happening in Mississippi, she answered that there had been loss of life in some of her churches, and thus much sorrow, but that during the hurricane churches had been sheltering people and sending out rescue boats. "I've not heard anyone ask, 'Where was God?' I've heard many say, 'God was with us.' . . . We have all levels of sadness but also a tremendous sense of God's presence."[2] When we cooperate with God in meeting human need, we are answering the "Where was God?" question by demonstrating God's presence.

Something pragmatic in my soul convinces me that I don't have to understand how things got the way they are. I don't really need to know why a tornado hits one house and skips another. In truth, this question belongs to the meteorologist, not the theologian. My business as a believer is to bring good out of the circumstances that come my way. If I am in the batter's box at a crucial point in the game, it isn't my business to argue that perhaps sixty feet, six inches is not the right distance from pitcher's mound to home plate. My task is to hit the ball when it comes to me. I can fuss over the rules of the game until the last out is announced, but this isn't a very effective way to play the game. I refuse therefore to follow such a course.

So what can you and I do to cooperate with the will of God? To begin with, we can recognize that we're capable of doing something and that God expects us to. Henry Sloane Coffin, for years the president of Union Theological Seminary in New York put it well in one of his prayers. He addressed God as one "who art beyond the grasp of our highest thought but within the reach of our frailest

trust"—an apt description of God's ability and our need—
then prayed that we might be "creators with Thee of a better tomorrow."[3] We need to begin here: God is powerful
beyond our imagining, and we are indeed frail, but there
is within our partnership the possibility always of "a better tomorrow." This was the mood of America's spiritual
ancestors at the Plymouth Plantation. William Bradford
reports, "So they committed themselves to the will of God
and resolved to proceed."[4] I am absolutely sure that this is
the place to begin: take inventory of God's resources and
ours, and on that basis commit ourselves to the will of God
and proceed.

What a difference this attitude makes! When we resign
ourselves to the idea that "everything has a purpose," we put
up a white flag of surrender. When we set our minds on the
character of God and on the resources of God, when we seek
to envision all that Jesus might have meant when he urged
us to pray for God's kingdom to come on earth, then we are
empowered to dream boldly. When we believe that we are
called to play a part in bringing God's will to pass, we begin
to draw on the energy of heaven.

A next step is to enlist the help of others. Pursuing
the will of God in an often unwilling world is sometimes
lonely business, but this is not a business for lone rangers.
The people of God are meant to work in community. This
means that we will convince and recruit—and that we will
gladly join others who are already leading the way in some
project or program. God needs a few who will initiate and a
great many who will gladly participate.

We should not be too exclusive in choosing our partners in the pursuit of God's will. Frederick W. Faber reminds
us that "the love of God is broader than the measure of our
mind."[5] Since God reads the heart, while you and I tend to

read political and theological and ethnic labels, God often uses persons you and I might overlook—or with whom we might even be somewhat uncomfortable. To cooperate with the will of God may mean to cooperate with people who, from our vantage point, are not themselves godly.

Consider some biblical for-instances. The writer of Second Chronicles reports, "In the first year of King Cyrus of Persia, in fulfillment of the word of the LORD spoken by Jeremiah, the LORD stirred up the spirit of King Cyrus of Persia." Because of that divine stirring, Cyrus issued an edict declaring his intention to "build him [God] a house at Jerusalem, which is in Judah"; and because of that assignment Cyrus appealed, "Whoever is among you of all his people, may the LORD his God be with him! Let him go up" (2 Chr. 36:22–23). I expect that the people of Judah viewed Cyrus as a pagan king, but he was about to cooperate in bringing God's will to pass; more than that, he was appealing to God's people to work with him to that end. Later King Artaxerxes cooperated with Nehemiah in Nehemiah's desire to rebuild the walls of Jerusalem. Nehemiah was vigorous—indeed, almost merciless—in purging his nation of any foreign influences but he sought and accepted Artaxerxes' help.

The prophet Isaiah said that the Lord spoke of Cyrus as "my shepherd, and he shall carry out all my purposes" (Isa. 44:28). The prophet's language is especially significant because in the Hebrew Scriptures the role of King David, the most beloved of Israel's kings, is described in the metaphor of a shepherd. Now the prophet Isaiah gives that title to Cyrus—not a king of Israel but a king whose nation rules over Israel. Cyrus's victories, Isaiah declares, happen because he is the Lord's anointed, "whose right hand I [the Lord] have grasped to subdue nations before him" (Isa. 45:1).

The prophets of Israel saw their nation as chosen by God to bring God's purposes to fulfillment, but those purposes were for all the earth's inhabitants—indeed, not only for human beings but ultimately for the rest of creation as well. Thus the prophets envisioned a world where

> The wolf shall live with the lamb,
>   the leopard shall lie down with the kid,
>   the calf and the lion and the fatling together,
>   and a little child shall lead them."
>
> Isa. 11:6

While it was Israel's calling to lead the way to such perfection, all nations were to be involved. The prophets declared that God was the Lord of all nations, at work in their histories as well as in the history of Israel.

The Hebrew Scriptures taught that God used some nations and persons in the unfolding of God's will, even when they were not consciously cooperating. This understanding had ancient, family roots. Joseph's older brothers sold him to slave traders in the hope of being rid of him forever. Instead, roughly two decades later, they found themselves in his presence once again, except that now he was second in command in Egypt, possibly the most powerful nation in the world at the time.

At this point Joseph took the role of a theologian: "I am Joseph your brother whom you sold into Egypt. And now, do not be pained and do not be incensed with yourselves that you sold me down here, because for sustenance God has sent me before you. Two years now there has been famine in the heart of the land, and there are yet five years without plowing and harvest. And God has sent me before you to make you a remnant on earth and to preserve life, for you to be a great surviving group. And so, it is not you who sent me here but God" (Gen. 45:4–8, Alter). Professor Robert Alter writes, "Joseph's speech is a luminous illustration of the Bible's double system of causation, human and divine."[6] God works with human agents—preferably with people like Joseph who is intentionally in league with God's purposes, but also at times with those like his brothers, who stumble their way into participation with the will of God.

I dare to believe that God has great numbers of unconscious allies in the unfolding purposes of our universe. I suspect there is an agnostic somewhere just now doing research on cancer, or Alzheimer's, or AIDS. He or she and I differ dramatically in our beliefs about God. But as he or she seeks relief for one of our world's ills, I believe that he or she is in that degree an ally in pursuing the will of God, and I thank God for him or her.

If I had been pastor of the village church in Amherst, Massachusetts, in 1865, I am sure I would have been uneasy about that woman in my parish named Emily Dickinson, and I would have mourned that she did not leave her house. I would not have guessed that nearly a century and a half later, other preachers would still be quoting Dickinson:

> I never saw a Moor—
> I never saw the Sea—
> Yet know I how the Heather looks
> And what a Billow be.
>
> I never spoke with God
> Nor visited in Heaven—
> Yet certain am I of the spot
> As if the Checks [tickets] were given.[7]

But while I believe that God has unwitting and even unwilling partners in the fulfilling of the divine will, from the brothers of Joseph and kings Cyrus and Artaxerxes to the present hour, the crucial issue for you and me is to find our place in the cooperative enterprise of bringing the will of God to pass. Sometimes we will do so by our prayers. Certainly we will do so by our social, political, and economic influence—all of which may be much greater than we realize or than we are willing to realize (because if we realized, then more would be required of us).

Sometimes it is by our influence on others. Consider this telling sentence in the often painful stories of the kings of Israel and Judah: "As long as the high priest Joiada was his [Joash's] advisor, he obeyed the Lord's will" (2 Kgs. 12:2, Knox). I venture that this is often the role, not only of a pastor, priest, or parent, but also of an executive assistant or of an elder partner. Persons are kept within the boundaries of God's will by the direction, conduct, and counsel of those around them.

Consider too the importance of what seems minor and even insignificant. We hail those occasions when the will of God comes to pass with banners flying, but for every such instance I estimate that there are ten thousand happenings unnoticed but divine, some of which prepare the way for the more obvious occasions. If Jesus pictured the kingdom of God as leaven in a lump, as salt, as a mustard seed, we should surely understand that even our smallest loyalties and our least moments of holy sensitivity can be kingdom exercises.

We, the people of God, need to make the will of God our daily concern, not regard it as a subject that surfaces only when something inexplicable happens or as something that involves only those persons who function in places of obvious authority. Rather, we can ask ourselves daily—yes, hourly—in what ways we may participate in bringing God's will to pass in this unwilling world.

Our most important role on this earth is to help the will of God to be fulfilled. We do not have to know when the kingdom of God will come. We do know, however, that we are participants in the kingdom. Indeed, God has paid us mortals the unique compliment of making us cooperating partners in the eternal enterprise. This is challenging and, in the best sense, frightening; but it is also wonderfully exhilarating. Like Frank Laubach, we can ask each morning in our time and place, "God, what are you doing in the world today that I can help you with?"

Chapter 8

THE WILL OF GOD AND FAITH

In the fall of 2008 the *Christian Century* reported on the "stubborn belief" of a Dallas pastor, Gerald Britt. Twenty years earlier he had lost an eleven-year-old son to scleroderma, a disease in which the layers of the skin grow hard and rigid—one of those diseases that seem all the more monstrous because it is so rare and so irrational. Then, in 2007, another of his sons was murdered. A week after that son's funeral, Britt learned that he had prostate cancer. At that point Britt acknowledged that he had no theological explanation sufficient for what he was experiencing. But he said, "I choose to stubbornly believe that God is good. The book of Psalms is punctuated throughout with these words: 'The Lord is good,' and there are no qualifiers. . . . I choose to stubbornly cling to that unqualified goodness— even when things that happen to me are not good."[1]

Twice Britt uses the adverb "stubbornly" to describe the way he is reacting to his experience. There is a noun for that adverb: "faith." And there are people who understand both the adverb and the noun—literally millions of them, living and dead.

The Bible records the experiences of a notable few. The stories are told, often with little adornment, in the Old Testament, but an unknown New Testament writer collects those stories in one grand recital in the eleventh chapter of Hebrews, giving us a chance to bask in their accumulated wonder and power. There is Abel, a man who does everything right and whose reward is to be murdered by his brother, Cain. There is Enoch, of whom we know nothing except that he "walked with God; then he was no more, because God took him" (Gen. 5:24). Abraham and Sarah left near-retirement to start a whole new life, not knowing where they were going. Moses, who got a head start in stubbornness because his parents defied the law to save his life, chose "to share ill-treatment with the people of God" rather than enjoying "the fleeting pleasures of sin" (Heb. 11:25), and we remember him now as emancipator and lawgiver. The list goes on, including people who suffered mocking and flogging, chains and imprisonment, stoning, destitution, persecution, torment: a group so impressive that the writer tells us that the world is not worthy of such. "Yet all these, though they were commended for their faith, did not receive what was promised" (Heb. 11:39). They were persons who sought above all else to do the will of God as they perceived it—but they never got what they were looking for.

What part does faith play in our understanding of the will of God or in how we deal with what is thrust upon us as "God's will"? What is the role of faith, if any, for the family whose home and all of its memories have been swept away by a flood or a tornado—or perhaps by an economic tsunami? What of faith when we are in pain—physical, emotional, or spiritual? Does the experience itself have anything to do with the will of God? If it does, how do I understand it and make good of it? Where is faith in all of this experience?

The primary role of faith as it relates to the will of God is *the understanding that it brings.* At first it probably seems illogical to look to faith as a source of understanding. Faith itself seems more of a right-brain exercise. Often a well-meaning person tells the wrestling soul, "You just have to have faith," and with that counsel brings the discussion to an end. But I am thinking of the kind of faith that, rather than closing discussion, helps us stay in the battle and sometimes helps us to ask still more questions.

There are two ways to ask, "Why?" There is the accusatory "Why?" that does not really want an answer, and the "Why?" that seeks understanding and infers that if we know *why*, maybe we can work together in bringing good out of what seems inexplicable. We sometimes hear (and use) the accusatory "Why?" as parent, spouse, or friend, with questions like "Why do you always have to act like that?" We do not expect an answer.

"Why?" is a good question if it keeps the conversation open, whether with God or with persons. An honest "Why?" keeps communication alive, while a silent walking-from-the-room brings communication to an end. Let me underline that an accusatory "Why?" is also a conversation-ender, because the accusatory question is more like a statement aiming for rebuke rather than discussion and understanding.

William Cowper, the eighteenth-century British poet, was a gifted poet and a person of great inner beauty, but he was also a person who wrestled with a demon of depression—depression sometimes so overwhelming that it would drive him to the verge of suicide. In time he became a man of profound faith, who with his friend and pastor, John Newton, he produced the iconic Olney hymns. Millions still know Cowper for his poem-hymn "There Is a Fountain Filled with Blood." Sometimes despair would sweep over Cowper in such torrents that his faith would be all but lost. With all of his struggles, Cowper had the stubbornness of faith. So he could write:

> Our unbelief is sure to err
> And scan Your work in vain;
> You are Your own interpreter,
> And You will make it plain.[2]

Unbelief will, of course, err in its reading of the events of life. Doubt has a good chance of understanding, because doubt continues to ask and to seek, but unbelief closes the door. Cowper had traveled these several intellectual and emotional roads a great many times. Now he had come to realize that ultimately only God can rightly interpret God and the works of God, and he was content to wait for God to make plain the plan, the divine will. Biographers say that this hymn was written in 1774, probably about six months after he attempted to take his own life. It may be the last hymn Cowper wrote, although he lived another twenty-five years. Last or not, it communicates the faith with which the poet and hymnist took hold of the struggles of his life, and the conclusions he reached regarding the will of God as he was experiencing it.

Faith seeks, first of all, to understand the will of God. Faith does not require accepting all that happens as the will of God, but it believes that God can use all that happens and turn it to ultimate good. Faith therefore *interprets* what happens—whether in one's personal life or in unfolding human history—to see, if possible, a pattern, some evidence of God's involvement. Faith may even get so presumptuous as to imagine the ways by which God might choose to become involved, although any such reasoning on our part is always open to errors large and small, since we see only a few of the elements with which God is working.

The search for understanding is honorable; it pleases God, and God rewards it. The search may scan God's work clumsily and erratically, but by its intentions it opens the possibility of light and prepares us for faith's second role in its relationship to the will of God: *faith empowers us to use what happens to us and to our world.*

This is part of what the writer of Hebrews is telling us about Israel's history. The road that Abraham, Moses, and the judges of Israel traveled was certainly not a direct, unimpeded one. They needed therefore to see how they could use the experiences of their apparently erratic journeys. So too with those who suffered stoning and being sawn asunder; they needed not only to interpret what was happening to them, but also how to turn their suffering and persecution to good. Faith does not lie down before life's circumstances as a helpless suppliant; faith seeks ways to turn circumstances into purpose.

Henry Sloane Coffin recalls a story that came to him from A. C. Benson. Benson told of a friend who had a series of "devastating calamities." A man who cherished the warmth of his home circle, he saw it swept away; his artistic work had been both his occupation and his fulfillment, but his work was taken from him at the point of his best achievement. He lost his fortune too, though this meant little to him. But Benson continued, "I remember that he said to me once, not long before his end, that whatever others might feel about their lives, he could not for a moment doubt that his own had been an education of a deliberate and loving kind, and that the day when he realized this, when he saw that there was not a single incident in his life that had not a deep and an intentional value for him, was one of the happiest days of his whole existence."[3]

Clearly, when someone speaks in the fashion of Benson's friend, you know that they are not interpreting life on the basis of next year's recovery of health or on an upswing in the stock market. This person's view is both longer and deeper. It is longer in that it looks to the next generation and even, daringly, to eternity. Such a person trusts that someone will learn from them, whether by precept or example, and believes that no human life should be judged on the basis of this life only—first, because our influence can be carried on in the lives we touch directly and indirectly, and beyond that, because we believe in a world to come. This view is deeper in that our ultimate measure is not in elections won, earnings accumulated, books written, or esteem received, but in the quality of the soul that at last we present to God. Finally spoken, the quality of that soul is the deep and real fact of each life and the only really significant measure of the time we spend on this earth. If therefore we have the faith to use what happens to us to contribute to the making of a better, more mature soul, we have done well.

I don't want to sound like an obscurantist, talking pie-in-the-sky-when-you-die, but I rail against judging faith and the will of God simply on the basis of next week's miracle or next year's turn of fortune. I believe deeply that what we learn during faith's current struggle may make us better business persons, teachers, athletes, or leaders. And this is inestimably more important than today's or tomorrow's prosperity. Some accounts will not be settled on this earth, and we are traveling in very good company if we are among those of whom it can be said, "All of these died in faith without having received the promises, but from a distance they saw and greeted them" (Heb. 11:13).

The apostle Paul appealed in his letter to the Romans, "Do not be conformed to this world, but be transformed by the renewing of your minds, so that you may discern what is the will of God—what is good and acceptable and perfect" (Rom. 12:2). Even earnest Christians are sometimes too easily "conformed to this world" in their evaluation of the will of God. They judge the events of life too much on the standards of prosperity and well-being. Rather, the will of God is to be found in what is good and acceptable and perfect. Of course we are not likely to get such an attitude toward life and circumstances unless we experience a renewing of our minds.

Faith empowers us to use what happens toward the good. It drives us to take hold of the circumstances of our personal lives or of general disaster and to turn them to profit. It believes that God can bring good out of evil, even the worst of evil, and that since this is God's mind and purpose, we should seek ways to cooperate in that enterprise. Because we have faith, we do not stand on the sidelines waiting for God to impress us into divine service; we volunteer for the conflict.

Faith plays still another role in its relationship to the will of God: *It empowers us to hold on.* This is the stubbornness of faith. Faith believes that the game is not over until the will of God is done. Faith is not impressed by the scoreboard. Faith flies in the face of any time clock. Faith lives by its commitment to God's will, and it holds on to work with God to that end.

More than half a century ago Henry Sloane Coffin put it this way: "The call is for faith—assurance of things we ought to hope for because God hopes that they will come to pass."[4] Yes, it is for this reason that we hold on: we believe that there are things God hopes will come to pass, and we will not be satisfied until the will of God is fulfilled. If we are honest with ourselves, we will recognize the truth in Coffin's phrase "things we *ought* to hope for." I suspect that most of us do not hope for the purposes of God as faithfully as we should because we are not fully sensitive to God's purposes. We *ought* to be hoping for some matters that might well impinge on our own comfort because of what they might cost us—in money, or position, or influence. Faith will compel us to hold on. We *ought* to hope for some things that make us appear naive to a culture that insists that we have to be realistic and tough minded. We should, indeed, be tough minded, but tough minded in our readiness to keep hoping, praying, and working for the will of God in the face of all that seems hopeless and impossible.

This stubborn faith makes us respect the day of small things. Jesus taught us that his kingdom is a mustard seed, salt, and leaven sort of operation. You and I are sometimes so captured by the end picture of victory that we dream of great movements and of stirring miracles, not realizing that those miracles may come to pass through the small and the commonplace. God calls us to daily obedience. Several years ago I came upon a full-page advertisement in the *New York Times*. The headline was challenging: "What do you call someone who truly believes in Moshiach [Messiah] and expects the imminent Redemption of humankind?" The rhetorical answer was fascinating: *"A Realist."*[5] The advertisement made its appeal, concluding with a return coupon on which respondents could check ways in which they were ready to commit themselves to "additional good deeds." The responses were directed, of course, to Jewish readers—items such as "Giving my children a Jewish education," "Assisting the needy," "Keeping kosher,"

"Observing the laws of Jewish family life," "Doing more to treat my neighbors kindly."

Several things about this advertisement impressed me deeply. For one, that it appeared in a major secular publication. For another, that it dared to express such hope. But especially, that it spelled out its hopes in such modest steps. The return coupon was headed by a quote from the great Maimonides: "A single righteous act can tip the balance and make all the difference."[6] I pondered that a Christian could put together a comparable list, made up of just such simple, basic commitments—that, if faithfully, passionately, lovingly kept, might astonish us by the difference such "righteous acts," would make.

The burden upon us is to have faith enough in the will of God to commit ourselves to it, and, yes, to have faith enough in our place in the will of God to involve ourselves in its pursuit: daily, hourly, in all the commonness and wonder of life, in action and in prayer. Eugene Peterson reminds us of the quality of prayer. "Prayer is action," he writes. "Prayer is not a passive giving in to the way things are."[7] We are easily confused in this matter. Since prayer compels us to become submissive to the will of God, we sometimes equate the will of God with the way things are. Not so! Our present world is besieged by that which would thwart the will of God. The role of the believer is to contend for God's will in the face of that opposition. We dare not give in passively to "the way things are." Rather, we hold on doggedly to get things the way they ought, in the will of God, to be. Faith helps us in this holy doggedness.

So we find ourselves seeking the will of God in an unwilling world. Faith is absolutely essential in this enterprise. We are opposed on every side in our pursuit. The common philosophy tells us that we must take care of number one (and we know who that is), and such a concentration on self will not bring in the will of God. The continuing appeal of our culture is to sensate satisfaction, with little thought of the soul; so again the will of God is pushed into the background. Immediate fulfillment, hurry-up-please, is the mood of our world, when in truth almost everything that is worthwhile takes time and nurture. The will of God and the coming of God's kingdom, by contrast, seem in no hurry at all!

Those of us who pray often and earnestly for God's kingdom to come and God's will to be done are sometimes poor allies in bringing the will of God to pass. We are too ready to acquiesce to the evil that is in the world, too ready to give up, too quick to say of the difficult and even of the ugly that "it must be God's will." We are slow to keep before us the image of the good, the holy, the lovely, and the blessed.

We need a constant invigorating infusion of faith. We need the stubborn conviction that God is good and that we therefore will not surrender the will of God in this unwilling world.

Chapter 9

THE WILL OF GOD AND OUR INDIVIDUAL WORTH

I understand my personal worth primarily from what the Scriptures have taught me. Some of this has come directly, from my own reading—reading that began early, because I made my first Genesis-to-Revelation trip when I was eleven years old. But as much or more has come indirectly, from my parents and the culture in which I was raised, from pastors and evangelists and Sunday school teachers and self-appointed advisors. I read early that I was "fearfully and wonderfully made" (Ps. 139:14), and when I learned that my fingerprints are unique (and learned later that so too are my footprints, my knee and elbow prints, and my voice print), I saw this as evidence of the unique wonder of my person and understood it as God's declaration of my singular importance in heaven's sight.

Because of those who influenced my Christian life, this sense of worth was no ego trip. My own importance was not at the price of others. I was taught early and often that every human being is precious in the sight of God, with the same uniqueness I experienced. I have a special place in God's plan, but so does every person. What each of us does with the potential trusted to us is our role in the eternal equation of life's meaning.

With the passage of time I have become acquainted—like most of us—with the world of statistics. I know that the population of our world is numbered in the billions, and that each time I take a breath, great numbers of persons on this planet are taking their first or last breath. I know that hundreds of millions go to bed hungry each night, and that more persons than I can imagine are brutalized daily by political and economic systems and by unthinkable human cruelties. I do not know who first said that "life is cheap"—perhaps it was Cain, as he killed his brother Abel (Gen. 4)—but I know that many people say that life is cheap today with acts of mass destruction, mass indifference, and mass precision of oppression, so that it has become a more demonic statement than ever before in human history.

In the face of such statistics, what does the will of God have to say about our individual worth? Do we humans—we *individual* humans—really matter? Are we as expendable as the ants that work their way through a break in the concrete, only to be stepped on unintentionally by the morning jogger? Does God care what happens to us, what we think and dream and pray for and hope for? In the massive structure that we call the "will of God," does the individual matter? More specifically (for we cannot help but think this way, and in a sense we ought to), do you and I matter, and the people we know and love best?

Sometimes people answer this question in a peculiarly negative way. When some arm of nature capriciously takes one life or family while leaving the family next door intact, or when an out-of-control car leaps over the curb into a group of pedestrians, killing just one, the families of the victims ask, "Why did God do this to our family?"—as if they were very special in God's plan, but in a negative way. This is a philosophy of life for some. They may not mention God, but the inference is there: "If anything bad is going to happen, it will happen to me." Even this sense of victimization is a peculiar form of importance, a kind of booby-prize outlook on life. These persons feel that the will of God is at work in the world, but that their particular place in the plan of God is bad.

Some people seem justified in feeling this way. Most of us have known some family or individual with what seems like far more than their share of pain or sorrow or personal tragedy. In truth, I am surprised at how few persons who have suffered truly Job-like tragedies have been inclined to see their troubles as sent by God. Many of them testify that God has brought good out of their problems, and only rarely do they blame God for what has happened to them. Generally, they seem to have used their misfortunes to go deeper in their faith journey. Like Jacob (Gen. 32) after he wrestled with the stranger, they are resolved that they will not let go until they have asked for and received God's blessing (Gen. 32:26–29).

Jesse Stuart survived a major heart attack when he was at the height of his career as a poet, novelist, and lecturer. He memorialized the months of his recovery in a remarkable book, *The Year of My Rebirth*. In counsel to others who experience such a life-and-death encounter, Stuart included this word: "There is every evidence of the 'Divinity that shapes our ends.' This is something we don't have to prove. We are on this earth for a purpose. The world itself didn't just happen without the Greater Power's laws and intent. Life didn't come into being without reason. All around us, we find evidence of a Divinity."[1]

I believe deeply that you and I are on this earth for a purpose. This purpose is very personal, and it is significant. We are part of a huge enterprise, spread out over expanses of time and geography and multiple areas of activity and concern. It would be easy, therefore, to see ourselves as simply cogs in an unfathomable machine. But cogs have no mind of their own; they simply perform the function for which they are made. You and I are not cogs. We not only choose whether or not to cooperate with the divine program; we decide the degree to which we will invest our energy for God's purposes, when we will do so, and how consistent we will be in participating.

I believe that each of our acts is important; indeed, that each thought is important, because it is in our thoughts that our actions are born. A few persons in positions of political, social, or economic power affect the lives of many. In our day an interesting phenomenon has developed: it is more and more common for entertainers and athletes to become beloved public figures who affect many lives. Thus thousands and perhaps even millions will mourn the death of an athlete or an entertainer. But all of us, no matter how famous, matter—and matter deeply. The act of touching even one life is significant if one believes that every life is uniquely significant to God.

Even though I believe that every life has a purpose, I do not conclude that this purpose will necessarily come to pass. Several things are against it. For one, as surely as we want our perception of the good to be accomplished, there is someone with a different plan in mind. They may have a different understanding of what is good, or their vision may be selfish and, in some instances, even demonic. But we should be perceptive enough to know that our vision too can be clouded by selfishness or by a lack of depth or breadth. At the same time our neighbor's vision, while it seems at cross purposes with our own, is probably as well intentioned as our own. We may come to realize, in hindsight, that it was a good thing that the purposes of others interfered with our purposes. God's purpose is entirely right, but by the time God's purpose is filtered through your personality or mine, its purity is likely to be tainted.

The purposes of God in an individual life may be frustrated by circumstances only indirectly related to the individual. I still think of a man I will call Earl Brown. When I knew him, roughly sixty years ago, he had a routine job in a factory office in the second shift, a job that did not require much of an education. But Earl spent every weekday morning in the public library, reading—simply because he loved learning and loved to discuss ideas. Earl should have been a teacher. With his love of knowledge and his capacity to communicate, he would have brightened any classroom. But the economic realities of the Great Depression wasted these particular talents God invested in him. I cannot be content with the idea that it was God's will for Earl's particular talent to go unused. We learn from one of Jesus' parables that our Lord does not think well of folks who bury their investment in the ground. I cannot believe therefore that God is pleased for any of the divine investment in our human personalities to suffer such waste—not necessarily because of the individual's wasting it but because of the times and circumstances that control our lives. Our Lord resents such misuse and expects us to do what we can to set it right.

Each of us has a significant place in the plan and purpose of God, and because God has entrusted the daily operation of our lives and this world to us, we can either further or impede God's activity. God has made it to be so; we are the caretakers of the present and contributors to the shaping of the future.

All of us, in some measure, are caught in the maw of large matters—war, economic depression, cultural movements—that can delay the larger purposes of God and all but quench the best potential of particular individuals.

Barely half a century ago, cultural structures prevented many women and racial minorities in this country from achieving their full potential as doctors, professors, and policy makers. Activists, people of faith, have done much to change discriminatory situations, and yet full equality still is not a reality for everyone.

Even if we are prevented by circumstances, we are human beings and not cogs in a machine. We have no right to use the circumstances as an excuse to absent ourselves from the game entirely. If prevented in one area, a human being continually must look for another place to make his or her mark.

If we take seriously the Scriptures—and the pages of human history—we will realize that what may seem insignificant to us is quite possibly crucial. Cheri Cowell, a contemporary inspirational writer, asks, "Why do we worry so much about the big decisions in life and spend so little time on the little day-in-and-day-out decisions? Could it be that the character we build in making little choices for God's way develops the habits that turn mountains too difficult to surmount into molehills easily traversed?"[2] An old proverb warns, "For want of a nail the shoe was lost; for want of a shoe the horse was lost; for want of a horse the rider was lost." Some versions add, "For want of a rider, the battle was lost; for want of a battle, the kingdom was lost." The historian would add, "An age was lost." In a sense, there is no day of small things.

This kind of thinking can become very subjective, to our peril. I am uneasy when I read Thomas Merton's report of the time when he was struggling with French translations of hundreds of Eastern texts. He was finding them baffling and uninteresting. Then a Hindu monk directed him to the Christian mystical tradition. Later Merton wrote, "Now that I look back on those days, it seems to me very probable that one of the reasons why God had brought him all the way from India, was that he might say just that."[3] I hesitate to say, as Merton did, that God has maneuvered the life of another person to accommodate some development in my life. I am more than ready to thank God for the way some of the pieces of my life come together and for the people who helped make this happen, yet I back off from saying that God was intervening to make it so. Perhaps I am drawing a fine line. Nevertheless I could not help wondering if some who read Merton's account with enthusiastic approval would be as receptive if an eccentric person down the street, without Merton's credentials, reported having a similar experience.

Even with all these cautious statements, I declare gladly that I believe that God is indeed at work in our lives, often in matters that are relatively insignificant to anyone but the person or persons involved. Since I am convinced that God has chosen to make us co-workers in the eternal enterprise, I believe God honors us still further by bringing minor miracles and mysteries into our otherwise commonplace journey.

Some persons have vocations in which their daily work provides obvious channels for the purposes of God. I say this hesitantly, because I do not want to rule out God's purposes in anyone's task, but some assignments seem to me to be especially sensitive. One of the most notable is also one of the most commonplace, and therefore one easily taken for granted: parenthood. When I speak of parenthood, I would quickly extend its boundaries to include teaching—especially at the elementary, middle school, and high school levels—as well as leadership in programs like scouting. Any of us who are trusted with the upbringing of children and young adults, whether by parenting or daily work, are in a strategic place to shape the future for the kingdom of God.

I think too of research scientists, who by their sometimes tedious daily assignments push back the boundaries of pain and destruction. This is the work of God, whether the person so engaged realizes it or not. Blessed are such workers if they realize the divine partnership in which they are engaged! They work on the edge of divine revelation every day.

I feel the same potential in the dedicated legislator: the unpaid member of the local school board, the city council representative, the state legislator, and those in national government or in the United Nations. Politics at best is a study in compromise and at worst is "dirty business." But given a chance and used rightly, it is also the way of statesmanship, something very near to the task of the Hebrew prophet.

I am thinking just now of a towering figure from the mid-twentieth century, Dag Hammarskjöld. As the son of a former prime minister of Sweden, he grew up in a world of learning and sophistication. A brilliant economist, he became the youngest chairman of the Bank of Sweden in the bank's history. He was thrust upon the world scene in 1953 when he became secretary-general of the United Nations. In that role he worked to bring understanding between the United States and Russia, brought about the release of American soldiers who were imprisoned in China following the Korean War, and helped solve the Suez crisis that involved not only Egypt and Israel but also France and Great Britain. He was killed in a plane crash in Africa in 1961 while trying to negotiate peace in the Congo. Some months later he was awarded the Nobel Peace Prize posthumously.

Hammarskjöld saw his work as a divine assignment. His entries in his private journal, published after his death, make this clear. He believed that in our era, "the road to holiness necessarily passes through the world of action." Often, of course, he found it a lonely road. Thus he wrote, "Didst Thou give me this inescapable loneliness so that it would be easier for me to give Thee all?" His work made him walk in the most demanding and exalting corridors of power, but he saw himself not simply under the command of nations and their leaders, but more certainly under God. "I am the vessel," he confided to his journal. "The draught is God's. And God is the thirsty one."[4]

If you and I have any measure of self-perception, we will feel altogether out of our league in comparing our role in bringing the will of God to pass. But Hammarsjköld would be the first to speak otherwise. "The 'great' commitment all too easily obscures the 'little' one. But without the humility and warmth which you have to develop in your relations to the few with whom you are personally involved, you will never be able to do anything for the many."[5]

A life such as Dag Hammarsjköld's encourages us to know that still in our times God has servants in what the culture sees as "high places." It also reminds us that the cost of pursuing the will of God increases as the issues grow more demanding. The will of God involves the affairs of nations and the unfolding and redemption of history, and it also includes the concerns of a parent who wants the best for a child and the teenager who hopes to choose the right college. The God who refers to the ancient potentate Cyrus as "my shepherd, and he shall carry out all my purpose" (Isa. 44:28) is the same God who notes the sparrow's fall (Matt. 10:29).

My emphasis on what we can do to affect the kingdom of God and sometimes to influence community, national, and world affairs can make us forget that the kingdom of God is finally measured not in political dynasties but in personal character and in the destiny of our souls. Thus Jesus told a crowd, "This is indeed the will of my Father, that all who see the Son and believe in him may have eternal life" (John 6:40). Earthly kingdoms rise and fall; you and I, meanwhile, are called to be part of the kingdom of God, which is eternal. So here is the will of God, ultimately, for you and me: that we believe in Christ and have eternal life.

We are agents of the kingdom, so the quality of our lives influences the activity of God's kingdom in the present age. The apostle Paul, writing to a congregation of persons who expected that Christ might break in at any moment to bring his kingdom, gave them some very practical counsel having to do with some very practical matters—namely, their sexual fidelity. Paul's word to them about the will of God was this: "For this is the will of God, your sanctification" (1 Thess. 4:3). I suspect that this is a quite good place for all of us to begin any thought about the will of God in our lives and our personal worth in the purposes of God: God wants us to be *sanctified*. God desires purity of character and of conduct, primarily because we are creatures made in the divine image, and therefore we ought to try to live up to that inestimable potential. Beyond that, God desires purity of character and conduct so that we can be forces in our world to bring in God's kingdom: sometimes by little measures (as we see it) each day and sometimes, whether we know it or not, by effecting issues and achievements altogether beyond our imagining.

You and I are persons of exceeding personal worth—in our own right and in our place in the will of God.

Chapter 10

THE WILL OF GOD IN
OUR PERSONAL LIVES

Any attempt to discuss the will of God as we experience it
has to range from the eternal to the momentary, from the
history of nations and the shaping of empires to a person's
choice of a job, a school, or a life partner. I say this because
this is the way we speak of the will of God in our own experience, and this is the way it is treated in the Scriptures.

So I turn now to this sparrow's view of God's will,
the issues of daily life that seem of little consequence com-
pared to the rise and fall of empires or even the life and
death of individuals. Does God care so intimately about
the issues of our daily round that we should inquire of the
divine mind in our hours of decision? Or is it arrogant to
think that God has time for such details? When one of my
students is offered a position in a given church and asks that
I pray for her to know the will of God, should I pray with
her regarding her choice, or should I encourage her simply
to use her own good judgment?

The Scriptures of both the Old and New Testaments make clear that we humans instinctively seek God's
will; more than that, the Scriptures put a seal of approval
on such conduct. Consider the story of Gideon. When he
was called to lead Israel at a time of national crisis, he felt
a need for reassurance and asked God to give evidence of
the divine will. He laid a fleece of wool on the threshing

floor and asked that, if God confirmed his call, there be dew on the fleece but the ground all around be dry. When this happened, Gideon reversed the request: dry on the fleece and wet on the ground. "And God did so that night" (Judg. 6:40). The biblical writer indicates no divine impatience with Gideon's request—a procedure, incidentally, that has given a code phrase to many devout persons, who speak of "putting out a fleece" when they seek to know the will of God for some personal decision.

Israel's priestly leadership had what seems like a rather mechanical device, one that modern readers will see as tending to the magical. The high priest, Aaron, was to have in his "breastpiece of judgment" the Urim and the Thummim, sacred lots to guide in making decisions (Exod. 28:30). Robert Alter suggests that they probably "generated a binary response to whatever question was posed: yes or no, guilty or innocent."[1] The Urim and Thummim were worn by Aaron at his ordination (Lev. 8:8), and Moses made special reference to them in the prayer before his death (Deut. 33:8). Both Ezra and Nehemiah reveal the trust they placed in these symbols in their reports of the reestablishing of Israel in its homeland following the Babylonian-Persian captivity (Ezra 2:63; Neh. 7:65).

The early church used a method not very different from the Urim and Thummim. After Jesus' resurrection and ascension, one of the first acts of his followers was to find a successor to Judas, so that the disciples would again number twelve. They set up a standard: the person must have been one of Jesus' followers from the earliest days of his ministry. From this group they picked two, Justus and Matthias. Then they prayed, asking God's guidance, and "cast lots for them, and the lot fell on Matthias; and he was added to the eleven apostles" (Acts 1:26).

Some persons, noting that Matthias is never heard from again, criticize the early church for this action. But neither do we read more about some of the other original Twelve, like Thaddeus and Bartholomew. The church began their search with a logical standard: the successor to Judas must be someone who had been part of their company from the beginning. Then the disciples resorted to something like the drawing of straws—or to something rather like the Urim and Thummim from their Jewish heritage.

Our judgment on the use of the Urim and Thummim and the casting of lots is not really very consequential. We live in a different time, which is surely not more devout or more understanding of the purposes of God than theirs, and perhaps not even more intellectually astute. When one sees the mixed results in our laborious choice of denominational leadership—or what happens sometimes in corporations and educational institutions after months of consultation and research—one thinks somewhat wryly that maybe we would have been as well off if we had drawn straws. My point now is simply that the Scriptures teach that God is concerned with the affairs of our day-to-day existence and that heaven is not offended by such inquiries.

In the book of Acts, the guidance of God's Spirit seems to be a given. Paul and Timothy and Silas are "forbidden by the Holy Spirit to speak the word in Asia." When they attempt to go into Bithynia, "the Spirit of Jesus did not allow them." The writer of Acts does not tell us how the Spirit communicated these insights. A more specific, more clearly mystical event came during the night when "Paul had a vision: there stood a man of Macedonia pleading with him and saying, 'Come over to Macedonia and help us.'" So they set out "immediately" for Macedonia, "being convinced that God had called us to proclaim the good news to them" (Acts 16:6–10). We are not specifically told that Paul and his team were asking for guidance in all of this process, but I think it can be assumed. They lived in a faith climate in which their dominant goal was to be aligned with God and God's purposes, so the will of God was always their goal, either explicitly or implicitly.

The succeeding centuries of church history are crowded with stories of believers seeking the will of God, fretting lest they have missed God's will, setting out on tasks with the conviction God is leading—journeys that sometimes have produced miracles small and large and that in other instances have ended in disasters embarrassing to the participants and to the work of Christ. I am very sure that God has a purpose in our individual lives and wishes to guide us in varieties of decisions, but I am admittedly uneasy with our human capacity for receiving and understanding God's will. Perhaps this is the between-the-lines element in the record of Paul's guidance to which I have just referred. When Paul says that he was checked in his travels, perhaps he is acknowledging that he set out on such directions thinking he knew the plan of God (perhaps he had even declared as much to Silas and Timothy) and that the checking was a kind of divine rebuke to his first ventures. I trust God's Holy Spirit. I am not as confident of the receptive accuracy of our own spirits.

Dietrich Bonhoeffer was a scholar who lived out his remarkable faith among both scholars and everyday believers. He warned against waiting "for direct inspirations," because, in doing so, we "all too easily" open ourselves to self-deception. He warned further of "the fanatical expectations and assertions of direct inspirations." But he continued, "There will be faith that God certainly reveals his will to anyone who humbly asks him. And then, after all earnest testing, there will also be the freedom to make a real decision."[2]

Bonhoeffer offers proper advice. I am very uneasy with those who treat the will of God and guidance as if they have a divine trip guide. Some of the language I hear in such instances seems more presumptuous and self-congratulatory than devout. Probably the average believer is at the other extreme, not concerned enough with the will of God. I am impressed that Alcoholics Anonymous has as the eleventh of its twelve steps, "Sought through prayer and meditation to improve our conscious contact with God, as we understood Him, praying only for knowledge of His will for us and the power to carry that out."[3] I am also impressed that persons I've known who have been especially faithful in following the program testify that the most demanding and important step in spiritual growth is a true concern for discovering and carrying out the will of God in one's own life.

Most of the decisions of our daily lives are, in fact, routine, and God expects us to handle them with the intelligence and judgment we already possess. When I was young, I asked a man whose saintly wisdom I greatly admired, "How do you find the will of God?" I expected an extended statement. He answered, "Providence. When a door opens, I walk through it." There was an underlying assumption: if we are seeking to live rightly, by God's will, we can be confident that the doors that open are of God. I find essentially the same mood in God's word to Israel through the prophet Isaiah: "And when you turn to the right or when you turn to the left, your ears shall hear a word behind you, saying, 'This is the way; walk in it'" (Isa. 30:21).

But what if we are at a place in life that seems a dead end? What if there is no open door, indeed, no further path and no exit—only a maze that seems to have no meaning or purpose? Edwin Lewis, that fine twentieth-century philosophical theologian, gave a pragmatic answer: "We can regard the inevitabilities of life as the will of God for us."[4] I vote for this pragmatism because I see nothing to be gained in railing against life's circumstances unless one can and will do something about them. I offer this counsel to the church worker who is frustrated in a particular calling and in frustration asks if this place is God's will. I insist on that worker employing himself or herself as if the task is God's will for as long as he or she is in that place. If the negative feeling is so strong that the worker cannot be honorably employed, then he or she can be unemployed in the will of God. But as long as one is in a place of service, one must treat it as God's place and God's will.

At the same time I remember Henry Sloane Coffin, as he discussed how our lives can sometimes be hedged in. "We are never to call our limitations God's hedge," he wrote, "until we are sure that neither we nor others can remove them."[5] And sometimes it is the hedge itself that blesses life. Coffin recounts how the writer Victor Hugo sent his clothing out of the house while he was writing *The Hunchback of Notre Dame* because he feared he would be tempted to go out before he had finished the book.[6] We must not make peace with untoward circumstances until we are sure we cannot change them. If we cannot change them, we must use the circumstances themselves to further the will of God, toward the goodness and beauty and hope and salvation our world needs.

Suppose in some past decision or action I have missed the will of God. Suppose that by either my stubbornness or my inability to see God's will I have made a disastrously wrong choice—in my education, my marriage, my choice of career, or decisions made within my career—what then?

If I have missed the will of God, must I (and others) pay for my mistake all the rest of my life?

J. I. Packer, the esteemed Canadian theologian, notes that some people see God's plans for our lives as an itinerary drawn up by a travel agent: if we miss one connection, the trip is ruined. You can get a revised plan, but it will always be second best. Not so, Packer insists. That kind of thinking assumes that God lacks either the will or the wisdom or both to get us back on the right road. God is better than that.[7]

I agree emphatically. God is better than God's plans—at least, as we perceive those plans. No matter how sincere you and I may be in seeking the will of God, we are always limited by our humanness. We are not only short sighted; we have our own spiritual myopia. Because of the influences at work in our lives, we often see the second rate as excellent, the transient as permanent, and the acceptable as holy. We make our choices accordingly. Often we do so with great earnestness, meaning to honor God by what we do. Years later we join in the ancient lament, "If only I had known then what I know now."

In truth, the will of God, as most of us experience it in our personal lives, is a moving target. This is not because of any uncertainty in God or in God's purposes but because of our actions. Fortunately, God is able to "adjust" to our moving; and fortunately, God moves faster than we do.

I can dare to say that God is more important than God's will, and God is bigger than God's will. God's will, as you and I deal with it, is filtered through our human perceptions and is skewed by our deeds and words. So God is forced constantly to work not with virgin soil but with the soil we make by our arrogance, our tentativeness, our rebellion, our poor understanding, and our fumbling with the data of life.

But God is not defeated by this. As I look at the history of Israel in the Old Testament, the brief history of the church in the book of Acts, and the unfolding of history both sacred and secular since then, I have to conclude that God is not discouraged by what happens. Instead, God adjusts. Did I choose the wrong school in light of my career potential? Then God, in ways both mundane and mysterious, blessed me in that school with a special teacher, a particular company of friends. Have I made mistakes that shadow my reputation? So did Saul of Tarsus, so that some could never forgive him. But it was from these errors that Saul became Paul the apostle with unique capacity and insight. In truth, if God did not use our mistakes, our second-rate decisions, our misuse of the assigned plays, God would have very little, if anything, with which to work.

Our role is to continue seeking God's will in our lives and make peace with the mysteries—sometimes agonizing mysteries—of life. At the same time, however, we need to ask, How can I do something about the circumstances I face? It is our responsibility and our privilege to deal with, adapt to, and seek to understand the unfolding circumstances.

You and I are the only ones who can frustrate, complicate, or delay the will of God in our lives. Others can add to our misery or can make our task more difficult—just as they also can help us expedite God's will, often more than we know. But we stand alone with God at the point of final decision. If we choose badly, we must remember that this does not defeat God. God not only has a Plan B for our lives; I venture there are also Plans C through Z, and then starting through life's alphabet yet again.

The greatest barrier to the will of God in the lives of some very sincere Christians may be their undue preoccupation with God's will. In their earnest desire to do what is right, they forget that God is also concerned for their welfare and that they can go to sleep and leave something to God.

Thomas Merton handled this matter perfectly. He began his prayer by confessing, "I have no idea where I am going." Then he continued with a prayer all of us can endorse: "Nor do I really know myself, and the fact that I think I am following your will does not mean that I am actually doing so. But I believe that the desire to please you does in fact please you. And I hope I have that desire in all that I am doing. I hope that I will never do anything apart from that desire. And I know that if I do this you will lead me by the right road, though I may know nothing about it."[8]

I cherish Merton's acknowledgment that thinking I am following God's will does not mean that I am actually doing so; that confidence can easily slip into spiritual arrogance. I am profoundly comforted and strengthened by Merton's further noting, "But I believe that the desire to please you does in fact please you." I am grateful for the pleasure God takes in our best desires. Those desires may sometimes be poorly shaped and even more poorly carried through, but God rejoices in their earnest existence.

Let us not forget the holiness factor. In all of our earnest seeking to find the will of God in the issues of our lives, the will of God for each of us is our sanctification (1 Thess. 4:3). The day-to-day decisions in which we seek God's guidance are important, but not as important as our growth in faith, our sanctification. And our sanctification often finds its most fertile prospects in the soil of our sins and failures. This too is grace. When we discuss the will of God, we ought never to forget God's grace.

Chapter 11

THE WILL OF GOD
AND THE KINGDOM OF GOD

If we intend to work with the will of God, we must be ready to work with the long view. We cannot deal with the issues surrounding the purposes of God if we live only with today. The subject of God's will compels us to have both a sense of history and a spirit of hope. It is quite impossible to understand today without remembering something about yesterday. In truth, much of the time I find it hard to understand even today in the light of yesterday; I do better understanding yesterday in light of the day before yesterday. I get my context for understanding God's will for today as I review what happened yesterday and the day before. I need the long view: the memory of what God has done in other times and the faith to throw myself into the even longer challenges of the future.

With the stability and perspective that come from our knowledge of the past, we need to keep an eye on tomorrow. More than that, we need to put a foot into tomorrow. When we catch a true vision of the will of God, we become a special kind of optimist, and we are stimulated by the long view. We know that today is never the conclusion of the story. Today may be a grand step or a faltering one, but it is always only a step, a unit of unfolding. As Henry Sloane Coffin said, "Christians early learned not to look for the completion of their hopes on earth." Coffin grieved that his generation in the mid-twentieth century had dropped the words "pilgrims and strangers" from the vocabulary of faith, the capacity for seeing ourselves as a people "moving towards a better country where God's purposes arrive."[1] Our generation may well know these words only as a kind of fascinating curio. This is why we find it difficult to understand and to build faith in a God who *wills*, a God of purpose and continuing activity.

This brings us back to the prayer our Lord gave us. Listen again:

> Your kingdom come.
> Your will be done,
>   on earth as it is in heaven.
>   Matt. 6:10

When we speak of the will of God, we are entering the mind-set of God's kingdom. This kingdom is immediate—we are living in its demands and its fulfillment this very day—but it is also breathtakingly long range, as long range as the perfection of heaven. How do we know the will of God is being done? Because we see God's kingdom in action. To what degree has God's kingdom come? To the degree that God's will is being done.

This is why any thoughtful discussion of the will of God requires the long view. Most of us know those instances in our own lives or in the lives of friends where the tragedy or the confusion of the day before yesterday becomes plain and meaningful today. In the biblical story of Joseph, his dreams crashed when his brothers threw him in a pit and sold him into slavery. They crashed still further when Potiphar put him in prison. There was a moment of hope when Joseph interpreted a dream for the king's cupbearer; but when the cupbearer forgot Joseph, the hope was deferred and Joseph's pit became an abyss. Only many years after Joseph's brothers had disposed of him did Joseph come to his place of fulfillment, the place where at last the will of God was clear and evident.

What is true at an individual level is also true in the patterns of human history. Herbert Butterfield, the brilliant professor of modern history at Cambridge University, put it half playfully: "Perhaps history is a thing that would stop happening if God held His breath, or could be imagined turning away to think of something else."[2] In 1862 Abraham Lincoln wrestled with a nation that had broken asunder, where lives were being sacrificed by the thousands. With no end in sight, Lincoln wrote in a private musing, "The will of God prevails. In great contests each party claims to act in accordance with the will of God. Both may be, and one must be, wrong. . . . In the present civil war it is quite possible that God's purpose is something different from the purpose of either party—and yet the human instrumentalities, working just as they do, are of the best adaptation to effect his purpose."[3] Some three years later, in his second inaugural address, Lincoln declared, "The Almighty has His own purposes." Lincoln did not venture to interpret God's purposes, but he spoke with a truly biblical sense of the will of God as he continued, "Yet if God wills that it [the war] continue until all the wealth piled by the bond-man's two hundred and fifty years of unrequited toil shall be sunk, and until every drop of blood drawn with the lash shall be paid by another drawn with the sword, as was said three thousand years ago, so still it must be said, that the judgments of the Lord are true and righteous altogether."[4] Lincoln was expressing the long view, a view demanded of those who seek the will of God. It was not, at that moment,

a comfortable view, but it was in the best sense of the word
a *faith* view, because it contended for God's judgment in
righteousness.

In our search to discover and to understand the will
of God, we must hold constantly to the conviction that evil
is not the last word—nor is the street-slang synonym for
evil, "bad luck." These words are issues that we have to
deal with, simply because the ideas are so much with us
that they easily influence our thinking. Dietrich Bonhoeffer lived at a time when many of the best intellectual and
political leaders of his nation were following a course that
seemed to much of the rest of the world to be a course of
madness. Much of the Christian leadership in his nation
was acquiescing in this evil. It looked as if the lights were
going out in Germany and that darkness was in control, but
Bonhoeffer insisted that "in the resurrection we know the
will of God for a new world."[5] In the face of evil Bonhoeffer
contended for the resurrection, God's ultimate sign of the
victory of righteousness over evil, and he dared to declare it
as "the will of God."

Bonhoeffer died, of course, without seeing even the
transient victory of God's will in Hitler's defeat. There are
questions about the will of God that almost surely we will
not be able to answer. At such points I choose to believe in
the goodness of God and in the strength to concentrate on
what you and I can do to help shape the answers.

In the daily struggle for the will of God in our world,
I find strength in two quite different responses. I resonate
to the indomitable vigor of G. A. Studdert-Kennedy, the
Anglican rector and World War I chaplain who continued
to minister with a passion in London for a decade before
his untimely death, dedicating himself much of the time
to what seemed like hopeless causes. I am in awe of his

untiring expectation that the will of God would be done in this world and the next. Looking through the clouds of Calvary, he wrote, "I believe that Evil dies, / And Good lives on, loves on, and conquers all."[6]

There is another, quite different mood with which to hold steady for the will of God. The prophet Jeremiah did so through tears: "You will be in the right, O LORD, when I lay charges against you; but let me put my case to you" (Jer. 12:1). He pleaded for God to be fair in what seemed to him an utterly unfair time. Gerard Manley Hopkins recast Jeremiah's complaint for himself: "Thou art indeed just, Lord, if I contend with thee; but, sir, so what I plead is just."[7] There are quite different ways by which we can question God. There is the questioning that searches for a sustaining faith, and there is the questioning that seeks simply to register our complaints. Jeremiah and Hopkins were troubled, perhaps even bewildered, by the will of God as they were experiencing it; but they argued the matter with God because they were certain God was better than what they were currently experiencing. They were holding out for a further development in the will of God. So should we all. The kingdom of God is among us, Jesus said (Luke 17:21); yet it is a kingdom whose fulfillment Jesus constantly urged his followers to seek.

This brings us again to the tension between the sovereignty of God and our participation in the will of God. Ultimately God is the issue and the arbiter: it is the will of *God* that we are discussing. Eugene Peterson reminds us that "kingdom" is "a metaphor for a world that is ruled by a sovereign, and that when we pray 'Your kingdom come,' it is implicit that God has never abdicated this throne. It is a sovereignty that invites our participation. We share his rule, but it is *his* rule."[8] Jesus tells his disciples, "Do not be afraid, little flock, for it is your Father's good pleasure to give you the kingdom" (Luke 12:32). However, it is painfully evident that we are not very good at receiving this gift.

God has chosen to limit his own authority in order to work with us human beings. When we complain that God seems indifferent to our sense of time and seems never to be in a hurry, we need to ask if perhaps the delay is in us rather than in God. So Peter, writing to a generation that was already becoming impatient with God's timing, said, "The Lord is not slow about his promise, as some think of slowness, but is patient with you, not wanting any to perish, but all to come to repentance" (2 Pet. 3:9). In light of the times, Peter asks, "What sort of persons ought you to be in leading lives of holiness and godliness, waiting for and *hastening* the coming of the day of God?" (2 Pet. 3:11, emphasis added). If the will of God is slow in coming to pass in our world, we must ask ourselves whether we are the impediment. The purposes of God can be hastened, and we are the agents of hastening.

At this point we might learn from an ancient Sufi tale. The Muslim emphasis on submission may help to correct the sense of independence that seems natural to many of us. In this story a seeker went everywhere to find authentic religion. At last he found a group of people who were honored for the sincerity of their service, the singleness of their hearts, and the goodness of their lives. Impressed, the seeker raised a question: "Does your God work miracles?" One of the devout answered, "It all depends on what you mean by a *miracle*. Some people call it a miracle when God does the will of people. We call it a miracle when people do the will of God."[9]

Some of us get in the way of the will of God through greed or ambition or love of power. These are facts from the world of economics and politics and human nature. These facts operate not only among dictators and in corporate offices, but also in local school boards and in the places where we ordinary folks choose to invest our money. We cannot control the natural disaster, but we can determine what safeguards we will build and what we will do to relieve the sufferings of the disaster victims. We humans do not yet understand the mysteries of cancer, but we already know enough to protect ourselves and others from some of the more obvious causes, and we also have the power to make present remedies more widely available. It is irrational to blame God for the tragedy caused by a distracted or drunken driver. It is almost blasphemous when someone explains such heartbreak by saying, "It must have been God's will," or "It was just their time to go." Rather, we need to confront our human involvement in the world of pain and to do what we can, where we are, to eliminate or relieve that pain.

Until God's kingdom finally and completely comes, we will have to rewin some battles in every generation. The field of conflict may differ slightly, but the issues of the conflict will be the same: time vs. eternity, self-interest vs. love, greed vs. generosity. We often say that we do not need to reinvent the wheel; I wish the same could be said in our struggle for following the will of God. In the world of automobiles, refrigerators, and computers we seek always (though not always perfectly) to build upon the progress of those who have gone before us. But in issues of morality and ethics the battle has to be rewon in every generation, sometimes in new areas of conflict and sometimes, to our shame, in battles as old as our human race. This is because in the most important matters we are individuals rather than machines, and as such we choose for ourselves.

History tells us clearly enough that selfishness destroys, but selfishness is appealing enough that we insist on learning the lesson for ourselves in each new generation.

Then, too, times and circumstances change. More than half a century ago, Henry Sloane Coffin wrote, "No perfect plan will be devised for the re-ordering of the economic life of our race. Were a plan forthcoming which would appear satisfactory today, it would require revision tomorrow, for circumstances are ever shifting in this always changing human society."[10] While circumstances change and specific remedies grow obsolete, basic convictions remain unchanged. Justice and peace are as right today as they were in the days of the Psalms. Poverty is as much an evil as when the law of Moses insisted on the rights of the orphan, the widow, and the alien. New occasions do not so much teach new duties as compel us to face the duties that have always been ours, and to face them in ways appropriate to the times in which we live. The kingdom of God is *now*, and must be lived *now*, in the midst of computers and progress and heartaches and need.

So what is the sum of the matter? I end where I began, with the conviction that the will of God for us is always good. It has been since Eden, since the sense of perfection that affirms itself in every human heart. God's will was good in the struggles of Noah, Abraham and Sarah, and Moses. God's will for good was declared unforgettably in the Hebrew prophets and then most particularly in the life, death, and resurrection of Jesus Christ.

God has given us humans a strategic place in the fulfilling of God's will. We can be coworkers in bringing God's will to pass, or we can be accomplices in delaying it. Some of those who cooperate with evil in obstructing the will of God do so intentionally (though they probably do not reckon God into the equation), in their greed or prejudice or unthinking malice.

However, the most effective opposition to the will of God comes from those of us who do nothing. We would not think of allying ourselves with evil—not knowingly, at any rate. But in the face of evil and of need, we are preoccupied with our own concerns. Worse, we have sometimes opted out of the conflict on theological grounds. We have found it too easy to say, "It must have been the will of God," when we should have asked ourselves if perhaps "an enemy has done this" (Matt. 13:28).

So much of the pain in our world is homemade. So many of life's tragedies—including those that are passed on from one generation to the next—are the result of our human choices, including the choices of those of us who fail to involve ourselves on the side of righteousness. Not many of us will have the opportunity to produce legislation or medical research that will go down in history for making life better on our planet, but every one of us has opportunities every day to bring the love of Christ into someone's life. Even if we do not see another human being, do not write a note or an e-mail or make a phone call that day, we can shape the business of eternity by our prayers. In this world, where so many cast a vote against the will of God by action or inaction, you and I can cast our vote in favor of God's will.

What of the evil that is beyond our control—the sickness still incurable that strikes someone we love, the irrational accident, the eruption of nature? I will not call these matters the will of God until there is irrefutable evidence to show that it is. Meanwhile, I must do everything in my power to help the ones in need. The pain that I cannot prevent I must at least alleviate.

Let me underline one more time the importance of prayer. I cannot escape the fact that our Lord made the *will of God* a major petition in the prayer he gave his followers. I agree emphatically with Eugene Peterson when he writes, "Prayer is action. Prayer is not a passive giving in to the way things are."[11]

I want to be part of the company of those who are working for the kingdom of heaven. I want to join the noble body of Abraham, Sarah, Moses, and Rahab, who never got to see the kingdom but who pursued it; and of the saints and martyrs, known and unknown, who have worked since Calvary to see Christ's kingdom come. I vote with them rather than with the cynics and naysayers and the unduly cautious. Even if such persons remain a majority, they will never take the day. The victory is with Christ.

I cherish a dream, a dream that more and more of us will realize that when we pray, whether alone or in the company of God's people, "Your kingdom come, your will be done, as in heaven, so on earth," we ourselves must be the beginning of the answer to that prayer. Those words, "Your will be done," are nothing less than a declaration of war against all that is not God's will. They are the marching orders for the kingdom of God on earth, as in heaven.

NOTES

CHAPTER 1: WHEN EVERYONE IS A THEOLOGIAN

1. Lynn Johnston, "For Better or Worse," *Lexington Herald-Leader*, May 26, 2007, G-5.

2. William Safire, "Where Was God?" *New York Times*, January 10, 2005. http://www.nytimes.com/2005/01/10/opinion/10safire.html

3. *The Random House Dictionary of the English Language*, Jess Stein, editor-in-chief (New York: Random House, 1966), 1471.

CHAPTER 2: A WORLD OUT OF JOINT

1. Joseph Heller, *Something Happened* (New York: Alfred A. Knopf, 1966, 1974), 3.

2. Dietrich Bonhoeffer, *I Want to Live These Days with You* (Louisville, KY: Westminster John Knox Press, 2007), 30.

3. Ibid.

CHAPTER 3: OUR UNWILLING WORLD

1. Eugene Peterson, *God's Message for Each Day* (Nashville: J. Countryman, 2004), 135.

2. Adolf Eichmann, "Eichmann's Own Story: Part II," *Life Magazine*, December 5, 1960, 146–61; quote on 146.

3. Blaise Pascal, *Pensées* (New York: Modern Library, 1941), 314.

4. Lewis quoted in William Griffin, *Clive Staples Lewis: A Dramatic Life* (San Francisco: Harper & Row, 1986), 100.

5. *Encyclopedia of Religion in American Politics*, ed. Jeffrey D. Schultz, John G. West Jr., and Iain MacLean (Phoenix: Oryx Press, 1999), 146.

6. Cathleen Falsani, interview with Studs Terkel in "God-stuff," blog posted January 6, 2006, at http://falsani.blogspot.com/2006_01_01_archive.html.

7. Ibid.

8. Arthur Miller, *Arthur Miller's Collected Plays* (New York: Viking Press, 1957).

9. J. B. Phillips, *Day by Day with J. B. Phillips* (Peabody, MA: Hendrickson Publishers, 2003), 161.

10. Margaret Pepper, *The Harper Religious and Inspirational Quotation Companion* (New York: Harper & Row, 1989), 394.

CHAPTER 4: WHEN GOOD COMES OUT OF EVIL

1. Robert S. Gottfried, *The Black Death: Natural and Human Disaster in Medieval Europe* (New York: Free Press, 1985), 133.

2. John Julian, OJN, *The Complete Julian of Norwich* (Brewster, MA: Paraclete Press, 2009), 5.

3. Darryl Tippens, *Pilgrim Heart* (Abilene, TX: Leafwood Publishers, 2006), 195.

4. John Wesley, *Wesley's Notes on the Bible*, Christian Ethereal Library, http://www.ccel.org/ccel/wesley/notes.i.ii.viii.html.

5. Kathleen Norris, *Amazing Grace* (New York: Riverhead Books, 1998), 29

6. J. B. Phillips, *Day by Day with J. B. Phillips* (Peabody, MA: Hendrickson Publishers, 2003), 164.

CHAPTER 5: JESUS AND THE WILL OF GOD

1. Geoffrey A. Studdert-Kennedy, *The Best of G. A. Studdert-Kennedy* (London: Hodder & Stoughton, Ltd., 1947), 51.

CHAPTER 6: THE WILL OF GOD AND PRAYER

1. http://www.cyberhymnal.org/htm/w/s/wsirtmyg.htm.
2. Walter Brueggemann, "Letters," *Christian Century,* July 11, 2006, 44.
3. Charles J. Chaput, quoted in "The Up Side," *Guideposts,* March 2005, 17.

CHAPTER 7: COOPERATING WITH THE WILL OF GOD

1. Frank Laubach, "Letters by a Modern Mystic," in *Christian Spirituality*, ed. Frank Magill and Ian McGreal (San Francisco: Harper & Row, 1988), 516–20.
2. Hope Morgan Ward quoted in "Ministry through the Storm," *Christian Century*, October 4, 2005, 21.
3. Henry Sloane Coffin, *Joy in Believing* (New York: Charles Scribner's Sons, 1956), 134.
4. William Bradford, *Of Plymouth Plantation* (Mineola, NY: Dover Publications, 2006), 63.
5. Frederick William Faber, "There's a Wideness in God's Mercy" (1854), www.cyberhymnal.org/htm/t/h/e/therwide.htm.
6. Robert Alter, *The Five Books of Moses* (New York: W. W. Norton & Co., 2004), 261.
7. Emily Dickinson, *The Complete Poems of Emily Dickinson* (Boston: Little, Brown & Co., 1960), 480.

CHAPTER 8: THE WILL OF GOD AND FAITH

1. Century Marks, *Christian Century*, November 18, 2008, 8.
2. William Cowper, "O God, in a Mysterious Way," *The Presbyterian Hymnal* (Louisville, KY: Westminster John Knox Press, 1990), 270.
3. Henry Sloane Coffin, *Joy in Believing* (New York: Charles Scribner's Sons, 1956), 117–18.
4. Ibid., 188.
5. Advertisement, *New York Times*, April 7, 2006, A-17.
6. Ibid.
7. Eugene Peterson, *Tell It Slant* (Grand Rapids: Eerdmans, 2008), 50.

CHAPTER 9: THE WILL OF GOD AND OUR INDIVIDUAL WORTH

1. Jesse Stuart, *The Year of My Rebirth* (New York: McGraw-Hill Book Co., 1956), 247–48.
2. Cheri Cowell, *In Me in You* (Wilmore, KY: Asbury Theological Seminary, 2009), 96.
3. Thomas Merton, *The Seven Storey Mountain* (New York: Harcourt and Brace & Co., 1948, 1978).
4. Dag Hammarskjöld, *Markings*, trans. Leif Sjoberg and W. H. Auden (New York: Alfred A. Knopf, 1964), vii–xxii.
5. "The Invisible Man," *Time*, October 23, 1964, 110.

CHAPTER 10: THE WILL OF GOD IN OUR PERSONAL LIVES

1. Robert Alter, *The Five Books of Moses* (New York: W. W. Norton & Co., 2004), 476.

2. Dietrich Bonhoeffer, *I Want to Live These Days with You* (Louisville, KY: Westminster John Knox Press, 2005), 143.

3. Alcoholics Anonymous, http://www.aa.org/en_pdfs/smf -121_en.pdf.

4. Edwin Lewis, *The Practice of the Christian Life* (Philadelphia: Westminster Press, 1942), 91.

5. Henry Sloane Coffin, *Joy in Believing* (New York: Charles Scribner's Sons, 1956), 128–29.

6. Ibid.

7. J. I. Packer, *God's Plans for You* (Wheaton, IL: Crossway Books, 2001), 81.

8. Thomas Merton, quoted in Henri J. M. Nouwen, *Encounters with Merton* (New York: Crossroad Publishing Co., 1972, 1981), 133.

CHAPTER 11: THE WILL OF GOD
AND THE KINGDOM OF GOD

1. Henry Sloane Coffin, *Joy in Believing* (New York: Charles Scribner's Sons, 1956), 68.

2. Herb Butterfield, *Christianity and History* (New York: Charles Scribner's Sons, 1950), 111.

3. Quoted in Ronald C. White Jr., "God Willing," *Christian Century*, March 8, 2005, 11

4. Abraham Lincoln, Second Inaugural Address, endorsed by Lincoln, April 10, 1865, March 4, 1865; Series 3, General Correspondence, 1837–1897, the Abraham Lincoln Papers, Manuscript Division, Library of Congress (Washington, DC: American Memory Project, 2000–2002), http://memory.loc .gov/ammem/alhtml/alhome.html.

5. Dietrich Bonhoeffer, *I Want to Live These Days with You* (Louisville, KY: Westminster John Knox Press, 2007), 129.

6. G. A. Studdert-Kennedy, *The Best of Studdert-Kennedy* (London: Hodder & Stoughton, 1947), 209.

7. Gerard Manley Hopkins, *God's Grandeur and Other Poems* (New York: Dover Publications, 1995), 50.

8. Eugene H. Peterson, *Tell It Slant* (Grand Rapids: Eerdmans, 2008), 174–75.

9. Joan Chittister, "Ministering to Those in Pain," *Christianity and the Arts Magazine,* Fall 1998, 17.

10. Coffin, 186.

11. Peterson, 50.